Baked Alaska

Recipes for Sweet Comforts from the North Country

Sarah Eppenbach

Illustrations by Mindy Dwyer

ALASKA NORTHWEST BOOKS™
Anchorage • Seattle • Portland

To Barbara Mery Bennett Oakie

*Thank you, Mother, for raising us to know the
pleasure of family and friends around the table
and the joy of preparing wonderful food.*

Library of Congress Cataloging-in-Publication Data
Eppenbach, Sarah.
Baked Alaska : recipes for sweet comforts from the north country / Sarah
Eppenbach
p.   cm.
Includes Index.
ISBN 0 88240-492-X
1. Desserts. 2. Baking. 3. Cookery—Alaska. I. Title.
TX773.E56   1997   97-10544
641.8'6—dc21   CIP

Originating Editor: Marlene Blessing
Managing Editor: Ellen Wheat
Editor: Cynthia Nims
Designer: Elizabeth Watson
Illustrations: Mindy Dwyer

Ginger Crinkles recipe from *The Fiddlehead Cookbook,* Copyright © 1991 by
Susan Brooks, John DeCherney, Nancy DeCherney, and Deborah Marshall is
reprinted here by permission of St. Martin's Press Incorporated.

Alaska Northwest Books™
An imprint of Graphic Arts Center Publishing Company
Catalogs and book orders: P.O. Box 10306, Portland, OR 97210
800-452-3032

Printed on acid-free and chlorine-free paper in Singapore

Acknowledgments

Sincerest thanks to all those excellent cooks who kindly contributed recipes for this collection: JoAnn Asher and Margie Brown/Sacks Café, Mark Austin and Kim Elliott/Vagabond Blues Coffee House, Mary Bishop, Suzanne Bishop, Betsy Brenneman, Dorrie Brown, Judy Cooper, Gail Corbin/Lisianski Inlet Lodge, Judy and Jay Crondahl/Crondahls' Bed and Breakfast, Glorianne DeBoer, Kirsten Dixon/Riversong Lodge, Peter Fitzmaurice, Lee Grogan, Barbara Louise Head, Joe Hickel/The Hotel Captain Cook, Robbie Jayne Johnson, David Lesh/Gustavus Inn, Kate Marsh, Deborah Marshall and company/Fiddlehead Restaurant and Bakery, Kitty Mathers, Diane McBride/Kachemak Bay Wilderness Lodge, Rie Muñoz, Elaine Nathanson, Barbara Oakie, Elsie Pegues, Bob and Deanna Persons/Double Musky Inn, Barbara Prescott and Mark Wumkes/Bab's 5th Avenue Bakery, David Pruett/Hälsingland Hotel, Jean Rogers, Simon & Seafort's, Mary Beth Smetzer, LoAnn Swanson, Ann Symons, Carri Thurman/Two Sisters Bakery, Michelle Ward and Lisa Morley/Taku Glacier Lodge, and Linda Wild.

Thanks also to several individuals who pointed me toward excellent sources: Robert Ames, Suzanne Bishop, Ann Chandonnet, Linda Sievers, Bridget Smith, and Chip Waterbury.

I am grateful to these publishing companies, which gave permission to use previously published recipes: Alaska Northwest Books, for the recipe for Sourdough Soft Ginger Cookies from *Alaska Sourdough* and the recipe for Winter Blueberry–Cranberry Pie from *The Riversong Lodge Cookbook;* St. Martin's Press for the recipe for Ginger Crinkle Cookies published in *The Fiddlehead Cookbook;* David and JoAnn Lesh for the recipe for Grasshopper Pie from *A Week of Recipes from Gustavus Inn at Glacier Bay;* and Ken and Michelle Ward for the recipe for Dried Cranberry and Orange Scones from the *Taku Glacier Lodge Cookbook.* The recipe for Crystal Snow Jenne's Lemon Sherbet, previously published in the *Juneau Centennial Cookbook,* appears here with the permission of the authors, Jane Stewart, Betty Harris, and Phyllice Bradner, to whom I express my thanks. Also, the recipe for Tenakee Orange Pecan Bread, published in *Tasty Treats from Tenakee Springs, Alaska,* appears here with permission, with my gratitude.

I value the interest and support of Marlene Blessing and Ellen Harkins Wheat of Alaska Northwest Books, and the fine editing provided by Cynthia Nims. Mindy Dwyer of Anchorage captured the spirit of this book with her charming illustrations, and Betty Watson tied everything together with a delightful design; thank you both.

Thank you to Barbara Oakie, my mother, and to Katherine Marsh, my sister, two most valued and trusted cooks, who cheerfully helped with the testing. I'm sorry about all the recipes that didn't work out (especially the pumpkin ones). Thank you also to Elizabeth Rodolf, my niece, who helped as well.

To Larry Eppenbach, husband and companion, thank you for all that you are and do. I'm sorry about the extra 20 pounds.

Contents

Cookies and Bars

Cakes and Tea Breads

Pies, Cobblers, and Crisps

Baked Alaska and Other Frozen Desserts

Custards and Puddings

Alaska's Sweet Comforts

Starr Hill, our Juneau neighborhood for 25 years, has as a focal point a small children's playground known as the Chickenyard, so named because an order of Catholic nuns once raised chickens on the site. It is a shelf scraped out of the hillside, with swings, a slide, and a basketball hoop, and bordered on one side by a raised concrete wall at a comfortable height for sitting and balancing a plate on your knees. On summer solstice, the neighborhood gathers in the Chickenyard for a potluck. I loved the sight of all my Starr Hill neighbors streaming out of their houses and down the hill to the Chickenyard, carrying their casseroles and pies, their cookies and crumbles, while the children and dogs cavorted alongside.

I grew up on a dairy farm outside the town of Grass Valley in the Northern California gold country. Like country people everywhere, our Grass Valley neighbors marked important occasions, festive or sorrowful, with quantities of goods baked from the harvest of their gardens and orchards. My early culinary vocabulary included custards and puddings, cobblers, crisps, crumbles, betties, pies, and that most prized of all country desserts, strawberry shortcake, made with rich, sweetened biscuit dough patted into a pie pan and baked in a hot oven, then split horizontally, slathered with butter, and topped with iced berries and heavy cream.

When I married and moved to Juneau in Southeast Alaska, I adopted a town with a history not unlike that of my birthplace—a former gold mining center with small wood-frame houses built on hillsides, accessed by long flights of stairs—except that Juneau lies on salt water. People harvested salmon instead of beef. The desserts tended toward the American classics already familiar to me but based on a different harvest. As a child I spent many hot summer afternoons in shorts and tall rubber boots (against rattlesnakes), picking wild blackberries for my mother's pies and cobblers. I now gathered blueberries, huckleberries, and orange-red salmonberries and wore tall rubber boots against the rain. (There are no snakes in Alaska.) I learned to search for tiny beach strawberries, highbush cranberries, scarlet thimbleberries, and something called a nagoonberry, a raspberry-like creeper highly prized for pie and jelly—but shy! Among berry pickers in Alaska, proof of undying friendship would be sharing the location of a dependable patch of nagoonberries.

In Grass Valley, raspberries, my mother's favorite, arrived at our table in tiny market baskets, precious as rubies and nearly as expensive. We never squandered them in baked goods but savored them au naturel, lightly dusted with powdered sugar. In our Juneau neighborhood, raspberries escaped from garden confines and multiplied with abandon. The canes rambled down the back slope from our house, producing huge, pendulous fruits that required harvesting daily, with a bucket. My mother, artfully scheduling her Alaska visits to coincide with the raspberry harvest, would practically swoon with pleasure. Raspberry shortcake! Raspberry jelly! Raspberry cordial!

Alaskans love to come together and share good food. Cannery crews still pause for "morning mug-up," a traditional break for coffee and conversation over a plate of something sweet: doughnuts, perhaps, or warm chocolate chip cookies. In summer, the busy season, neighbors rally for impromptu beach picnics and potlucks. A birthday, a sunny day, relatives visiting, a big salmon caught—practically any excuse will do. Holiday meals in Alaska typically involve untidy assemblages of adults and children, dogs and cats; big extended families filling in for the parents and siblings hundreds or thousands of miles distant. The feast invariably concludes with a smorgasbord of desserts. And in the depth of winter, friends gather in each other's kitchens to stave off cabin fever with hot fudge sundaes or pecan pie. For some reason, sweets make the dark months easier to bear.

The desserts produced in Alaskan kitchens tend to mirror the cooks: casual, unpretentious, and reliable, but not without the occasional eccentric twist. (What could be more whimsical than Baked Alaska, the flamboyant assemblage of hot meringue and cold ice cream?) Alaskans can be trendy and sophisticated when the occasion arises—I know many amateur chefs who produce admirable genoise, tiramisu, and real puff pastry. But this book celebrates humbler fare: simple, pioneer desserts that can be achieved with little more than a measuring cup, a bowl, and a wooden spoon (although a food processor never hurts), and baked in such varied locales as wilderness cabins and fishing boats. Old-fashioned country desserts like cobbler and upside-down cake may be undergoing a renaissance in the Lower 48, but Alaskans have been baking and enjoying them all along.

After all, Alaskan cooks share an illustrious heritage of "making do." Miners and prospectors braving the overland trails to the Klondike gold fields hauled provisions to last one year. One recommended "outfit" included 350 pounds of flour, 75 pounds of sugar, 25 pounds of salt, 10 pounds of baking powder, and 80 pounds of "evaporated" fruits among the 1300 pounds of supplies. *The Alaska Cook Book,* published during the height of the 1898 gold rush, showed how to turn these staples into fruit pies and puddings, cobblers, shortcakes, cinnamon buns, and the inevitable brown betty—sweet, comforting desserts that could be baked in camp using an iron skillet or the nested tin pans in the standard Klondiker's kit. No substance proved more versatile than magical, bubbling sourdough, which could transform ordinary flour into any number of satisfying treats, including doughnuts. Even now, when airplanes routinely provision the most remote communities with fresh produce and dairy products, the typical Alaskan larder will include canned milk and cream, powdered buttermilk, canned and dried fruits, and bottled or frozen lemon juice—the trusted staples of the back-country baker.

Supermarkets in Alaska's larger cities and towns carry a wide array of fresh fruit today, even tropical exotics such as star fruit and mangoes. For Alaskans, though, the fruits of choice remain the ones that grow wild in virtually every clearing and on every slope from Ketchikan to Barrow and cost only the hours invested in picking. Most Alaskans pursue berry-picking as an excuse to escape into the outdoors, with the promise of pie at the end of the day. But others treat the annual gathering of fruit as serious business, measuring the progression of the season by the quantity of berries cached in the freezer for winter. Used alone or in combination, the many varieties of berries form the basis of Alaskans' favorite desserts. Rhubarb, a fixture in most North Country gardens, grows as large as elephant ears in the near-perpetual daylight of Alaska's summer, and pairs naturally with most wild berries in sauces, pies, and crisps. Enormous smiles greet the first rhubarb pies of the season, signaling as they do the imminent arrival of summer.

The recipes in this collection come from my own family recipe files, neighbors and friends, and a few favorite bakeries and restaurants in Alaska. Several come from country inns and wilderness lodges, where some of Alaska's best home cooking and hospitality can be found. I believe they represent a cross section of the good-tasting, homey desserts that Alaskans like to bake. As a genre, they respond positively to experimentation and substitution—for example, replacing one variety of berry with another or a combination of berries, fresh fruits with frozen, white sugar with brown, fresh milk with canned, or butter with margarine. Having grown up on a dairy farm, where butter was our business, I find it difficult to reach for what Julia Child refers to as "the other spread," but few people in Alaska share this affliction. Most of the recipes can be expanded or contracted to suit the occasion, the ingredients, or the size of the pan, and are forgiving of imprecise measuring. While many of these desserts make splendid finishers to a fancy dinner (the Chocolate Almond Torte, Sacks Café Dark Chocolate Pots de Crème, and Betsy Brenneman's incredible Tangerine Cheesecake come to mind), I enjoy these sweet offerings most at other times of day. Served at morning coffee break, brunch, teatime, or intermission in the video entertainment on a dark, snowy evening, they can be appreciated as they deserve: as the centerpiece and not just the finale.

In the summer of 1996, my husband and I left Alaska to make a new home in Washington's San Juan Islands, a location in which the two landscapes of my past, the rolling meadows of Northern California and the evergreen-fringed islands of Southeast Alaska, seem to converge into one. Looking back on our quarter century in Alaska, I perceive those years as one long, joyous potluck of blueberry pies and rhubarb crisps. For what stands out in any retrospective vision are the precious moments when good friends and neighbors sat together at a kitchen table, or on a deck, or in a cabin, or in a wheelhouse, or on a beach or mountaintop, and shared delicious foods they gathered and prepared with their own hands. In Alaska, such moments come often; they are the sweetest comforts of the North Country.

Scones, Muffins, and Coffee Cakes

Taku Glacier Lodge
Dried Cranberry and Orange Scones

The quintessential log cabin stands on a grassy slope above the Taku River, about 30 miles from Juneau, a stone's throw from Hole in the Wall Glacier. Built in 1923 as a fishing and hunting camp, the cabin and outbuildings subsequently belonged to the adventurous musher Mary Joyce, who traveled the 1,000 miles from the Taku River to Fairbanks by dogsled in 1936. Now owned by Ken and Michelle Ward of Juneau, Taku Glacier Lodge welcomes summer visitors who arrive by floatplane to share a meal and a bit of history in a North Country paradise inhabited by bald eagles, mountain goats, moose, and bears. The excursion begins with a flight over part of the 1,500-square-mile Juneau Ice Field and culminates with a banquet of salmon baked over an alder fire. Taku cook Lisa Morley developed these unusual dried cranberry and orange scones as a treat for their visitors.

Preheat the oven to 400°F.

Sift or stir together the flour, sugar, baking powder, and salt in a large mixing bowl. Cut in the butter until the mixture resembles coarse meal, and set aside. In another bowl, beat the eggs lightly and blend in the orange juice and vanilla. Add to the flour mixture, along with the cranberries and orange zest, and stir gently just until blended.

Turn the dough onto a floured surface and knead lightly for a few turns. Roll or pat the dough to a thickness of about 3/4 inch, cut out biscuit-sized rounds, and place the scones on an ungreased baking sheet. Bake about 15 minutes, until golden.

Makes 12 scones.

2 cups all-purpose flour
6 tablespoons sugar
2 teaspoons baking powder
1/2 teaspoon salt
1/2 cup cold butter, cut into
  small pieces
2 eggs
2 tablespoons orange juice
1 teaspoon vanilla extract
1/2 cup dried cranberries
1/2 teaspoon grated
  orange zest

Triple-Ginger Cream Scones

In the Alaskan tradition, workers pause for "mug-up," a coffee break accompanied by a sweet treat. Served with lots of butter and orange or ginger marmalade, these ginger scones make lively fare for morning mug-up at home. A food processor makes quick work of the recipe and produces a very accommodating dough.

Preheat the oven to 400°F. Lightly grease a baking sheet.

Place the crystallized ginger in the bowl of a food processor with 2 tablespoons of the sugar, and pulse until very finely chopped. Remove and set aside for topping. Without washing the bowl, process the fresh ginger slices with the remaining 3 tablespoons of sugar until finely minced. Add the flour, baking powder, salt, and ground ginger, and pulse to mix. Add the butter, and pulse until the mixture resembles coarse meal. Add the 1/2 cup of cream and the egg, and process until the dough forms moist clumps.

Transfer the dough to a lightly floured board and knead lightly for 2 or 3 turns. Pat or roll the dough to a thickness of 3/4 to 1 inch and cut into circles or wedges. Place the scones on the baking sheet, brush the tops with the remaining cream, and sprinkle with the reserved crystallized ginger and sugar mixture. Bake 15 to 20 minutes, until crisp and golden.

3 or 4 pieces crystallized ginger
5 tablespoons sugar
1/2-inch piece fresh ginger, peeled and thinly sliced
2 cups all-purpose flour
2 1/2 teaspoons baking powder
1/2 teaspoon salt
1/2 teaspoon ground ginger
6 tablespoons cold butter, cut into 1/2-inch pieces
1/2 cup heavy cream, plus 2 tablespoons for brushing the tops
1 egg

Makes 12 scones.

Orange Currant Scones

One summer, while updating my guidebook to Southeast Alaska, I stayed at a bed-and-breakfast overlooking Tongass Narrows in Ketchikan, in the southern part of the Panhandle. Typical for the time of year, the waterfront hummed with the frenetic activities of floatplanes, cruise ships, tugboats, ferries, and fishing boats. In the morning my hostess, LoAnn Swanson, a woodworker who began her career working on wooden boats in the Ketchikan shipyards, brought me a breakfast tray with these memorable orange-flavored scones.

Preheat the oven to 400°F. Lightly grease a baking sheet.

Sift or stir together the flour, sugar, baking powder, baking soda, and salt to thoroughly blend. Cut in the butter until the mixture resembles coarse meal, then stir in the currants and orange zest. Make a well in the center of the mixture and add 3/4 cup buttermilk all at once. Stir with a fork only until the dough barely clumps together, adding more buttermilk if necessary.

Turn the dough onto a lightly floured surface and divide in two. Gently shape and pat each half into a 1-inch-thick circle. Cut each circle into quarters or eighths, and transfer the scones to the baking sheet. Brush the tops with the remaining buttermilk. Mix the sugar and cinnamon and sprinkle on top of the scones. Bake for 15 to 20 minutes or until lightly browned.

Makes 8 large or 16 small scones.

3 cups all-purpose flour
1/3 cup sugar
2 1/2 teaspoons baking powder
1/2 teaspoon baking soda
1/4 teaspoon salt
3/4 cup cold butter, cut into small pieces
3/4 cup dried currants
Grated zest of 1 orange
3/4 to 1 cup buttermilk

TOPPING
1 tablespoon sugar
1/2 teaspoon ground cinnamon

Jean's Rich Blueberry Muffins

Muffins aren't just for breakfast in Alaska. Vehicles for whatever berries might be in season, they round out the contents of lunch boxes, picnic hampers, backpacks. A friend from Fairbanks keeps a basket of fresh muffins on the kitchen counter at all times, for noshing.

Jean Rogers, a Juneau children's book author and accomplished baker, likes to put these muffins in the oven so that they emerge just in time for dessert. Her dinner guests eat them piping hot and slathered with butter, scraping the papers for the last crumbs. She also makes a "guilt-free" version, using margarine and undiluted fat-free evaporated skim milk.

Preheat the oven to 400°F. Grease a 12-cup muffin tin or line the tin with papers.

Sift the flour with the baking powder and salt, and set aside. Cream the shortening with the sugar until light and fluffy, then add the eggs and milk and beat lightly. Stir in the dry ingredients, then the blueberries, mixing only enough to distribute the berries. The batter will be quite stiff.

Fill the muffin cups 2/3 full and bake 20 to 25 minutes. The paper will stick a bit when the muffins are hot but peel off cleanly when cool (if you can wait that long).

Makes 12 muffins.

2 cups all-purpose flour
1 tablespoon baking powder
1 teaspoon salt
1/4 cup vegetable shortening
1/3 cup sugar
2 eggs
2/3 cup milk
1 cup blueberries

13

Lemon Raspberry Muffins

Our Juneau house overlooked a vacant lot covered with raspberry canes during our early years there. I happily added raspberries to everything from shortcake to waffles, delighting in their intense flavor and color. The raspberries glow like rubies in these beautiful muffins. The lemon-sugar glaze adds a light sheen.

Preheat the oven to 400°F. Grease a 12-cup muffin tin or line the tin with papers.

Sift or stir together the flour, sugar, baking powder, and salt in a mixing bowl and set aside. Lightly beat the eggs in another bowl. Stir in the milk, melted butter, and lemon zest, and add this mixture to the dry ingredients. Blend just enough to incorporate most of the dry ingredients, then fold in the raspberries. Fill the muffin cups 2/3 full and bake for about 15 minutes, until golden.

While the muffins bake, stir the lemon juice and 1 tablespoon of sugar until the sugar dissolves. Let the muffins cool in the pan a minute or two, then remove and quickly dip the top of each muffin into the lemon-sugar glaze.

Makes 12 muffins.

1 3/4 cups all-purpose flour
1/2 cup sugar
2 teaspoons baking powder
1/2 teaspoon salt
2 eggs
3/4 cup milk
1/4 cup butter, melted
Grated zest of 1 lemon
1/2 cup raspberries

LEMON-SUGAR GLAZE
2 tablespoons lemon juice
1 tablespoon sugar

Cranberry Cornmeal Muffins

*T*art cranberries, which grow wild throughout Alaska, taste wonderful combined with cornmeal. These buttery muffins look beautiful in a breakfast basket but also pack well for the trail. Use either wild or cultivated cranberries, and substitute blueberries in summer.

Preheat the oven to 400°F. Grease a 12-cup muffin tin, or line the muffin tin with papers.

Sift the flour, cornmeal, sugar, baking powder, salt, and baking soda into a large mixing bowl. In another bowl, lightly beat the eggs. Blend in the buttermilk and melted butter. Add the mixture to the dry ingredients and stir quickly and lightly until just combined. Fold in the cranberries.

Fill the muffin cups 2/3 full and bake about 15 minutes or until lightly browned.

Makes 12 muffins.

1 cup all-purpose flour
1 cup cornmeal
1/2 cup sugar
2 teaspoons baking powder
1/2 teaspoon salt
1/4 teaspoon baking soda
2 eggs
1 cup buttermilk
1/4 cup butter, melted and cooled slightly
1 cup cranberries, coarsely chopped

Spiced Pumpkin Muffins

ith no regular access to fresh groceries, Alaskan bush cooks place a high value on recipes based on off-the-shelf ingredients. These gorgeous ocher muffins taste strongly of pumpkin. Not overly sweet, they can stand alone with butter and jam or do duty with soup and stew. I sometimes add chopped pecans to the cinnamon-sugar topping.

Preheat the oven to 400°F. Grease a 12-cup muffin tin, or line the tin with papers.

Sift the flour, sugar, baking powder, cinnamon, ginger, cloves, and salt into a large mixing bowl. In another bowl, beat the egg lightly, then stir in the pumpkin, milk, and oil. Add to the dry ingredients all at once. Stir only until combined, using a few quick strokes. Fold in the raisins, currants, or pecans. Fill the muffin cups 2/3 full.

For the topping, mix the sugar and cinnamon and sprinkle on top of the batter. Bake the muffins until lightly browned, about 20 minutes.

Makes 12 muffins.

1 1/2 cups all-purpose flour
1/2 cup sugar
2 teaspoons baking powder
1 teaspoon ground cinnamon
1/2 teaspoon ground ginger
1/4 teaspoon ground cloves
1/4 teaspoon salt
1 egg
1/2 cup pureed cooked
   pumpkin
1/2 cup milk
1/4 cup vegetable oil
1/2 cup raisins, currants, or
   chopped pecans

TOPPING
1 tablespoon sugar
1/2 teaspoon ground
   cinnamon

Banana Nut Muffins

Dependable bananas lend their wholesome sweetness to winter treats in most northern kitchens. These rich, tender muffins rise to every occasion.

Preheat the oven to 350°F. Grease a 12-cup muffin tin, or line with papers.

Sift the flour, sugar, baking soda, and salt into a large mixing bowl. Stir in the nuts. In another bowl, beat the egg lightly, then mix in the milk, banana, and butter. Add to the dry ingredients all at once, and stir only until combined. Fill the muffins cups 2/3 full and bake 20 to 25 minutes, until browned.

Allow the muffins to rest in the pan 3 to 4 minutes before removing. Dip the tops into granulated sugar and place on a rack to finish cooling.

Makes 12 muffins.

1 1/2 cups all-purpose flour
3/4 cup sugar plus additional
    for topping
1 1/2 teaspoons baking soda
1/4 teaspoon salt
3/4 cup chopped walnuts
    or pecans
1 egg
1/4 cup milk
3 ripe, medium bananas, well-
    mashed (1 to 1 1/4 cups)
6 tablespoons butter, melted

Joel's Birthday Coffee Cake

For several years in Juneau, we looked forward to the annual December birthday brunch that our friends John and Ann Symons hosted for their son, Joel. Naturally Joel got to choose the menu, which invariably included bagels and cream cheese, sausage, scrambled eggs, fresh fruit compote, and this light and tender coffee cake flavored with cinnamon and walnuts. Ann's mother clipped the recipe out of a newspaper some 40 years ago.

For this versatile coffee cake, you can add the sugar and nut mixture in one or two layers instead of on top, stir in a couple of cups of blueberries, or change the flavor with the addition of nutmeg or cardamom.

Preheat the oven to 350°F. Generously grease a tube pan.

Cream the butter with the sugar until light and fluffy. Add the eggs and vanilla, blend well, then stir in the sour cream. In a separate bowl, sift together the flour, baking powder, baking soda, and salt, and stir into the sour cream mixture. Pour the batter into the pan and smooth the surface.

Combine the sugar, nuts, and cinnamon for the topping and sprinkle over the the batter. Bake 45 to 50 minutes, until the cake tests done with a wooden toothpick. Cool in the pan for 10 minutes before removing to a rack.

Makes 12 servings.

1/2 cup butter
1 cup sugar
2 eggs, lightly beaten
1 teaspoon vanilla extract
1 cup sour cream
2 cups all-purpose flour
1 teaspoon baking powder
1 teaspoon baking soda
1/4 teaspoon salt

TOPPING
1/4 cup sugar
1/4 cup chopped walnuts
  or pecans
1 teaspoon ground cinnamon

Vagabond Blues Blueberry Coffee Cake

*W*hen Mark Austin moved north from Chicago, he tried commercial fishing and gold mining before he and partner Kim Elliott opened Vagabond Blues Coffee House in Palmer's historic Koslosky Center. They struck a chord in this fertile river valley settled by Dust Bowl farmers in the 1930s, where present-day growers produce record-sized cabbages for the annual state fair. This blueberry coffee cake, with a surprise lemon-ricotta filling, never lasts very long.

Preheat the oven to 350°F. Grease a 10-inch round baking pan.

Sift the flour, sugar, and salt into the bowl of an electric mixer. Using a pastry blender or two knives, cut in the butter until the mixture resembles coarse crumbs. Reserve 1/2 cup of the mixture. Add the milk, egg, baking powder, and vanilla to the rest of the mixture and beat on medium speed for 2 minutes. Pour the batter into the pan and distribute the blueberries on top.

Stir together the ricotta, egg yolk, sugar, and lemon zest until smooth. Spread the filling over the blueberries.

Combine the reserved crumbs with the almonds, brown sugar, and cinnamon, and sprinkle over the filling. Bake the coffee cake for about 35 minutes, until a wooden toothpick comes out clean.

Makes 8 servings.

1 1/4 cups flour
2/3 cup sugar
1/2 teaspoon salt
6 tablespoons cold butter
6 tablespoons milk
1 egg
1 teaspoon baking powder
1/2 teaspoon vanilla extract
1/2 cup blueberries

FILLING
1/2 cup ricotta cheese
1 egg yolk
1 tablespoon sugar
1/2 tablespoon grated
　lemon zest

TOPPING
1/2 cup reserved crumbs
1/4 cup finely chopped almonds
3 tablespoons brown sugar
1/2 teaspoon ground
　cinnamon

Mary Beth Smetzer's Buttermilk Cinnamon Rolls

*T*he Alaska Cook Book, *published in 1898 for prospectors bound for the Klondike, outlines the basic technique for baking cinnamon and raisin rolls from sweetened bread dough, fattened with lard and studded with currants or raisins. Alaskans still love cinnamon rolls. Mary Beth Smetzer, an editor with the* Fairbanks Daily News-Miner, *is famous among her friends and colleagues for these giant buttermilk specimens and has even baked them (six at a time, in a toaster oven) in a private home in Japan, while chaperoning a class trip. Her recipe makes two full pans, 24 large rolls. But rather than halve the recipe (easy to do), Mary Beth typically gives the second dozen away (really easy to do).*

Dissolve the yeast in the warm water and set aside. In a very large bowl, mix together the oil, eggs, sugar, and salt with a whisk. Add the buttermilk and dissolved yeast, and blend well. Start adding flour, 1 or 2 cups at a time, beating well with a wooden spoon and using your hands when the batter becomes too stiff to stir. When almost all the flour has been added, turn the dough onto a flat surface and knead for 5 to 10 minutes or until the dough becomes smooth and elastic. Place the dough in a large, clean bowl, cover with a clean dish towel, and set in a warm place to rise until doubled in bulk.

Punch the dough down, cut in half, cover, and allow to rest for about 10 minutes. Lightly butter two 12-by-17-inch baking sheets. Roll out half of the dough into a rectangle about 20 inches long and 1/2 inch thick. For the filling, spread with half the butter. Mix the sugar and cinnamon together. Sprinkle with half the cinnamon sugar and enough raisins to suit. Roll the dough into a cylinder and pinch together along the long edge. Slice into 12 rolls and space

Dough

2 tablespoons active dry yeast
1/2 cup warm water
1 1/3 cups corn oil
3 eggs
1 cup sugar
1 teaspoon salt
1 quart buttermilk, scalded
  and cooled
12 to 14 cups bread flour
  (about 5 pounds)

them apart on one of the baking sheets. Repeat with the remaining dough and filling. Cover the rolls with a dish towel and let rise until they have nearly doubled in bulk and filled up the spaces on the sheet.

Preheat the oven to 375°F.

Bake the cinnamon rolls for 16 to 20 minutes, until lightly browned, switching sheets between the top and bottom racks midway through the baking for even browning and baking. Meanwhile make the icing: Beat the cream cheese and milk or cream until light and blended. Add the powdered sugar to taste, then stir in the vanilla. Cool the cinnamon rolls for about 10 minutes before icing.

Makes 24 large cinnamon rolls.

FILLING

1/4 cup butter, softened
1 cup granulated sugar
  (or 1/2 cup granulated plus
  1/2 cup brown)
1 1/2 tablespoons ground
  cinnamon
About 2 cups raisins

ICING

8 ounces cream cheese,
  softened
2 tablespoons milk or cream
About 1/2 cup powdered
  sugar
1 teaspoon vanilla extract

Pineapple Coffee Cake

*F*ruit coffee cakes suit the informal Alaskan lifestyle very well. Simple and delicious, they can be stirred together quickly for breakfast, brunch, or dessert and baked in a variety of pans, including a cast-iron skillet. Crushed pineapple gives this coffee cake a chewy texture and a flavor similar to pineapple upside-down cake.

Preheat the oven to 350°F. Lightly grease and flour a 9-by-13-inch baking dish.

Drain the pineapple, reserving the juice. Cream the butter with the granulated sugar, beat in the eggs and vanilla, and stir in the pineapple. Sift or stir together the flour, baking soda, baking powder, and salt. Lightly stir these dry ingredients into the batter, alternating with the milk and 1/2 cup of the reserved pineapple juice. Pour the batter into the baking dish.

Mix the brown sugar and pecans for the topping and sprinkle over the batter. Bake until the cake pulls away slightly from the sides of the dish and tests done with a wooden toothpick, about 35 minutes.

Makes 8 servings.

1 can (20 ounces)
  crushed pineapple
1/2 cup butter
1 cup granulated sugar
2 eggs
1/2 teaspoon vanilla extract
2 cups all-purpose flour
1 teaspoon baking soda
1/2 teaspoon baking powder
1/2 teaspoon salt
1/2 cup milk

TOPPING
1/2 cup brown sugar
1/2 cup coarsely chopped
  pecans

Judy Cooper's Chocolate Chip Oatmeal Cookies

*O*n Sunday evenings our dear friend and neighbor Judy Cooper would climb the many stairs to our house for the 9 p.m. broadcast of Masterpiece Theatre, *accompanied by a small contingent of her red Siberian huskies. Often she would bring dessert: depending on the season, a blueberry or rhubarb pie, or a brown paper bag of chocolate chip cookies hot from the oven.*

These cookies have succored hundreds of Alaskans during Judy's 25-plus years in Alaska as a VISTA volunteer, recreation director, Trans–Alaska Pipeline laborer, artist, musher, kennel owner, and environmentalist. They have launched innumerable late-night ferry departures, energized skiing and hiking expeditions, sustained board meetings, and been auctioned at art and charity events. They're the best.

Preheat the oven to 375°F.

Sift or stir together the flour, baking soda, and salt, and set aside. Cream the shortening and sugars until fluffy and light, then mix in the egg, hot water, and vanilla. Stir in the dry ingredients, followed by the oats and chocolate chips, and drop the dough by spoonfuls onto ungreased baking sheets. Bake 8 to 10 minutes, until the cookies brown and flatten. Cool on the baking sheets a couple of minutes before removing.

Makes 5 dozen cookies.

VARIATION: Substitute 2 cups raisins or 1 cup raw sunflower seeds and 1 cup raisins for the chocolate chips.

1 1/2 cups all-purpose flour
1 teaspoon baking soda
1 teaspoon salt
1 cup vegetable shortening
1 cup brown sugar
1 cup granulated sugar
1 extra-large egg
3 tablespoons hot water
1 teaspoon vanilla extract
3 cups rolled oats
2 cups (12 ounces) semisweet chocolate chips

Fiddlehead Ginger Crinkles

*F*ew restaurants in Alaska enjoy as devoted a patronage as Deborah Marshall's Fiddlehead Restaurant and Bakery in Juneau. Established in 1978, this beloved cafe/jazz club/art gallery improvises on the full range of Alaska's fresh bounty, from winter-caught king salmon to spring-harvested fiddlehead ferns to summer berries. Happily, the bakery specialties—North Douglas Chocolate Cake, Eighteen Carat Cake, Fantasy Cookies, Reality Cookies—know no season. Of all the bakery items, none receives higher accolades than these ginger cookies. Some people like them soft and squishy in the center. Others prefer them crisp.

Preheat the oven to 350°F.

Cream the butter with the sugar in a large mixing bowl until fluffy. Beat in the egg and then the molasses. Sift together the flour, baking soda, salt, cinnamon, and ginger, and stir into the butter mixture. Form the dough into walnut-sized balls, dip them in sugar, and place, sugar side up, on ungreased baking sheets. Bake 12 to 15 minutes.

For soft centers, remove the cookies from the oven when they are puffed, very light golden brown, and cracked on top. For crisper cookies, bake 2 to 3 minutes more, until the puffed cookies have fallen and turned golden brown. Allow the cookies to rest 2 minutes before removing them from the pan to finish cooling on racks.

Makes 3 dozen cookies.

1 cup butter
1 3/4 cups sugar, plus extra
   for topping
1 egg
1/3 cup molasses
2 3/4 cups all-purpose flour
1 1/4 teaspoons baking soda
1/2 teaspoon salt
1 3/4 teaspoons ground
   cinnamon
1 3/4 teaspoons ground ginger

Lemon Squares

ven the famously casual Alaskan lifestyle occasionally demands a dress-up cookie. These dreamy, old-fashioned lemon bars—known in some places, entrancingly, as "Lemon Love Notes"—appear regularly on Juneau buffet tables during the winter Legislative season, but they can travel to summer picnics too. A food processor makes easy work of the shortbread base.

Preheat the oven to 350°F.

Place the flour, butter, and powdered sugar in the bowl of a food processor and process until the mixture resembles coarse meal. (Or, cut in the butter with a pastry blender or two knives.) Press the mixture into an ungreased 8-inch square baking pan and bake 15 to 20 minutes, or until lightly colored on top and gold around the edges. Cool on a rack while preparing the filling. Leave the oven set at 350°F.

For the lemon filling, beat the eggs until frothy. Gradually add the granulated sugar and beat until the mixture becomes light-colored and foamy. Beat in the lemon juice and zest. Stir together the flour and baking powder and add to the filling, combining well. Pour the filling over the shortbread base and return the pan to the oven for 20 to 25 minutes or until the filling is set.

Cool in the pan on a rack before cutting into 2-inch squares. Dust with powdered sugar before serving.

Makes 16 squares.

SHORTBREAD BASE

1 cup sifted all-purpose flour
1/2 cup cold butter,
    cut into 1/2-inch pieces
1/4 cup powdered sugar

LEMON FILLING

2 eggs
3/4 cup granulated sugar
5 tablespoons fresh lemon
    juice
Grated zest of 2 lemons
2 tablespoons all-purpose flour
1/2 teaspoon baking powder
Powdered sugar, for
    dusting bars

Capital School Cafeteria Cookies

Years ago, Juneau's Capital Elementary School (a beloved neighborhood school, now closed) provided students with a hot lunch served in the gymnasium cafeteria. Teachers as well as students rejoiced on the days when the meal included these giant, chewy, coconut–oatmeal cookies.

This recipe makes enough for a scout troop. You might want to halve the recipe or freeze part of the dough for later use.

Preheat the oven to 350°F.

Cream the butter with the brown and granulated sugars, then beat in the eggs and vanilla. Mix the flour, oats, coconut, baking powder, baking soda, and salt. Add to the creamed mixture a little at a time, stirring to thoroughly blend. Spoon the dough onto ungreased baking sheets, using 2 to 3 tablespoons of dough per cookie, spaced about 2 inches apart. Flatten slightly and bake for 10 to 15 minutes or until brown on top and bottom. Let the cookies cool 1 to 2 minutes on the baking sheet, then remove to a rack to finish cooling.

Makes 4 dozen 4-inch cookies.

2 cups butter
2 3/4 cups loosely packed brown sugar
2 cups granulated sugar
4 eggs
1 tablespoon vanilla extract
5 cups all-purpose flour
4 cups rolled oats
4 cups sweetened flaked coconut
4 teaspoons baking powder
4 teaspoons baking soda
1 tablespoon salt

Dorrie's Chocolate–Chocolate Chip Cookies

One sunny August evening, a number of friends and acquaintances boarded the Alaska ferry LeConte for the 7-hour run from Juneau to Tenakee Springs, on our way to a birthday celebration. We staked out chairs on the open-air solarium deck, from which we enjoyed an unobstructed view of the passing islands and distant glaciers and mountains. Ignoring the envious glances of other passengers, we spread out a potluck supper of lemon-grilled chicken, salad, fruit, and homemade bread. Dorrie Brown then unveiled these devastating cookies, which quickly disappeared. You will probably want to double the recipe.

Preheat the oven to 350°F. Lightly grease a baking sheet.

Melt 1 cup of the chocolate chips over low heat or in the microwave and set aside to cool. Sift or stir together the flour, baking powder, and salt. Cream the butter and sugar until light and fluffy. Beat in the egg and vanilla, mixing well, followed by the cooled chocolate. Stir in the dry ingredients, then the nuts and remaining 1/2 cup of chocolate chips.

Drop the dough by small spoonfuls, 2 inches apart. (The dough will be very soft.) Bake for 8 to 10 minutes. Cool the cookies for 1 to 2 minutes on the baking sheet and then transfer them carefully to a foil-covered rack. They will be very tender just out of the oven but will firm as they cool.

Makes about 30 cookies.

1 1/2 cups semisweet
   chocolate chips
1/2 cup all-purpose flour
1/4 teaspoon baking powder
1/2 teaspoon salt
1/4 cup butter
3/4 cup sugar
1 egg
1 1/2 teaspoons vanilla extract
1/2 cup chopped walnuts

Classic Chocolate Brownies

S oon after moving to Southeast Alaska, my husband and I succumbed to the usual temptation of buying a boat, and I discovered this curious fact: trolling for salmon (as opposed to catching them) gives a person an uncommon appetite for sweets. I find a pan of your basic brownies takes care of this situation and stows very conveniently aboard a sportfishing boat.

This well-worn family recipe makes classic, nut-filled brownies, not for those who like their brownies fudge-like or ultra-rich. But I sometimes stir a tablespoon of instant espresso powder into the dough. An 8-inch pan produces brownies about 1 1/4 inches thick; bake in a 9-inch pan for thinner bars.

Preheat the oven to 350°F. Grease and flour an 8- or 9-inch square baking pan.

Sift together the flour, salt, and baking powder; set aside. Cream the butter and brown sugar until light and fluffy. Add the eggs, chocolate, and vanilla, and mix thoroughly. Stir in the dry ingredients and nuts, and smooth into the pan. Bake 25 to 30 minutes or until the dough shrinks slightly from the edges of the pan and tests done near the edge but still moist in the center. Do not overcook. Cut into squares when cool.

Makes 16 brownies.

3/4 cup all-purpose flour
1/4 teaspoon salt
1/4 teaspoon baking powder
1/2 cup butter
1 cup brown sugar
2 eggs, beaten
2 squares (2 ounces) unsweetened chocolate, melted and slightly cooled
1 teaspoon vanilla extract
1 cup chopped walnuts or pecans

Pioneer Date Nut Bars

Early Alaska cooks relied upon dried fruits to sweeten and flavor their desserts and provide health-sustaining vitamins in winter. Local cookbooks of the period abound with recipes for date pudding, date-nut bread, and date cookies. These exceptionally easy, one-bowl bars work well with dried apricots, too.

Preheat the oven to 350°F. Grease a 9-by-13-inch baking pan.

Combine the dates and nuts with the 2 tablespoons of flour and set aside. Sift the remaining 3/4 cup flour, sugar, baking powder, and salt into a large mixing bowl. Make a well in the center and add the oil, eggs, and vanilla. Beat until smooth. Stir in the date/nut mixture and spread the batter in the pan—it will be a thin layer. Bake 25 to 30 minutes, until golden and shrunk slightly from the edges of the pan.

Cut into 2-inch bars while warm, but cool in the pan before removing. Dust lightly with powdered sugar.

Makes 24 bars.

APRICOT BARS VARIATION: Substitute 1/2 cup dried apricots for the 1 cup dates and use brown sugar in place of granulated.

1 cup chopped dates
1 cup chopped walnuts
 or pecans
3/4 cup plus 2 tablespoons
 all-purpose flour
1 cup sugar
1/4 teaspoon baking powder
1/4 teaspoon salt
1/2 cup vegetable oil
2 eggs
1/2 teaspoon vanilla extract
Powdered sugar, for
 dusting bars

Peanut Butter Cookies

With their penchant for outdoor activities in every season, Alaskans know the importance of choosing comfort foods with some nutritional value. These perennial favorites please all ages and make delicious energy-boosters for the trail, ski slope, or fishing boat.

Preheat the oven to 350°F.

Resift the flour with the baking soda, baking powder, and salt. Cream the peanut butter, shortening, granulated sugar, and brown sugar until well mixed and fluffy. Beat in the egg, and stir in the dry ingredients. Roll the dough into 1-inch balls and space them apart on ungreased baking sheets. Flatten the cookies with a fork, making a crosshatch pattern, and bake 10 to 15 minutes, or until lightly browned.

Makes about 3 dozen cookies.

1 1/4 cups sifted all-purpose flour
3/4 teaspoon baking soda
1/2 teaspoon baking powder
1/4 teaspoon salt
1/2 cup peanut butter, preferably crunchy
1/2 cup vegetable shortening
1/2 cup granulated sugar
1/2 cup brown sugar
1 egg

Ruth Allman's Sourdough Soft Ginger Cookies

When we first moved to Alaska, Ruth Allman, doyenne of sourdough, still gave tours of the House of Wickersham, her uncle's mansion on Seventh Street, high above downtown Juneau. Judge James Wickersham, who came to Alaska in 1900, served as Alaska's congressional delegate and worked tirelessly to achieve territorial status and then statehood. He died 20 years before that goal was finally achieved in 1959. After his death, Ruth opened the House of Wickersham to visitors, and her endearingly eccentric tours achieved legendary status in Juneau's infant tourism industry. The tour culminated at the dining table, where Ruth stirred up a bowl of sourdough batter and served "Flaming Sourdough Waffles," which she achieved by igniting a sugar cube laced with lemon extract.

Ruth learned about sourdough while operating a fly-in lodge with her husband, Jack. This recipe for Sourdough Soft Ginger Cookies comes from her handwritten cookbook, Alaska Sourdough. The dough rolls and cuts beautifully after chilling.

Sift together the flour, baking soda, ginger, cinnamon, cloves, and cardamom and set aside. In another bowl, cream the shortening with the sugar until light and fluffy. Add the molasses, egg, and orange or lemon zest and mix well. Mix in the sourdough starter and then the dry ingredients, using additional flour as needed to make a soft dough. Chill the dough, covered, for several hours.

Preheat the oven to 375°F. Grease 2 baking sheets.

Roll out the dough on a floured board to a thickness of about 1/8 inch and cut into 2- or 3-inch shapes. Bake for 10 minutes.

Makes about 5 dozen cookies.

3 cups all-purpose flour, more if needed
1 teaspoon baking soda
2 teaspoons ground ginger
2 teaspoons ground cinnamon
1 teaspoon ground cloves
1/2 teaspoon ground cardamom
1/2 cup vegetable shortening
3/4 cup sugar
1/2 cup molasses
1 egg
2 teaspoons grated orange or lemon zest
1/2 cup Sourdough Starter (see page 33)

Sourdough Starter

There are many different methods for making a sourdough starter. The most basic is to combine equal parts flour and water in a glass or ceramic jar and leave the mixture, loosely covered, at room temperature for a few days to allow the natural yeast to begin fermenting. Other formulas use potato water, yogurt, or baking yeast to start the fermentation. The most reliable method is to beg some sourdough starter from a friend or purchase a packaged starter mix. Once "going," sourdough needs feeding with flour and water every week or so.

Butterscotch Bars

hese sweet, chewy bars meet all the important criteria for cabin cooking: they require few ingredients, make up in minutes by hand, and mix in a single pot on the stove.

Preheat the oven to 350°F. Grease a 9-inch square baking pan.

Sift the flour with the baking powder and salt and set aside. Melt the butter in a medium saucepan. Add the brown sugar and cook, stirring, until the sugar dissolves. Remove from the heat, cool slightly, and beat in the egg and vanilla. Stir in the dry ingredients and the nuts. Spread into the pan and bake for about 20 minutes, until the dough shrinks slightly from the edges of the pan.

Cut into squares when cool.

Makes 16 bars.

1/2 cup all-purpose flour
1 teaspoon baking powder
1/4 teaspoon salt
1/4 cup butter
1 cup brown sugar
1 egg
1 teaspoon vanilla extract
1 cup chopped walnuts
  or pecans

Glorianne's Scørpa

Glorianne DeBoer stitches and bakes Norwegian. A daughter of Petersburg, a Southeast Alaska community settled by Norwegian fishermen a century ago, she grew up steeped in the traditions of the old country, baking beside her mother and fishing for halibut and black cod alongside her father. Now a home economist, and vice president of the Sons of Norway lodge, she instructs others in the arts of Norwegian stitchery and baking.

Scørpa is a traditional Norwegian "dunking cookie" and a staple aboard Petersburg's famous halibut fleet. A denser version of the trendy Italian biscotti, these Norwegian-style rusks are hard, slightly sweet, and flavored strongly with cardamom—ideal for dipping into a cup of very hot, very black coffee. I find them addictive. They keep for months in an airtight container.

Preheat the oven to 350°F.

Sift or stir together 4 1/2 cups flour with the cardamom and salt, and set aside. Cream the butter and sugar until light and fluffy. Beat in the eggs, one at a time, and stir in the dry ingredients alternately with the cream. The dough should be stiff enough to roll and shape; if not, sift in additional flour. With lightly floured hands, divide the dough into 3 portions. Roll and shape each portion into a cylindrical loaf 12 to 14 inches long, and transfer the loaves to an ungreased baking sheet. Bake for 30 minutes, until firm to the touch and very slightly colored.

Remove the loaves and reduce the oven temperature to 150°F. While they are still warm, slice the loaves crosswise into 1/2-inch slices. Arrange the slices on the baking sheet cut side down and return them to the oven to dry for 2 to 3 hours, turning at least once. Allow the *scørpa* to cool completely before packing in a storage container.

4 1/2 to 5 cups all-purpose
   flour
1 teaspoon freshly ground or
   2 to 3 teaspoons bottled
   ground cardamom
1/2 teaspoon salt
1 cup butter
1 1/2 cups sugar
3 eggs
1/4 cup heavy cream

Makes about 3 1/2 dozen cookies.

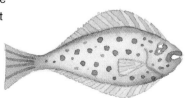

Chocolate Macaroons

*A*fter naturalist John Muir traveled into Glacier Bay by dugout canoe in 1879, his *accounts of the wondrous scenery prompted steamship companies to offer summer tours up Alaska's Inside Passage. The first, the steamer* Idaho, *came north in 1883, carrying a 27-year-old journalist, Eliza Ruhamah Scidmore. Alaska's visitor industry was launched. These early tourists glided through the raw-edged wilderness in surprising comfort, surrounded by plush carpets, crystal chandeliers, and starched linens. The several-course meals always concluded with a selection of desserts. Puddings and pies featured regularly on shipboard menus, as well as fancy layer cakes, fresh fruit ices, and chocolate macaroons like these.*

Preheat the oven to 300°F. Line a baking sheet with parchment paper.

Place the almonds and sugar in the bowl of a food processor and pulse to pulverize. Add the cocoa and salt, and pulse once or twice to mix. Add the egg whites and almond extract, and process until the mixture forms a soft, moist dough. Drop by spoonfuls, or pipe through a large star-shaped tip, onto the prepared baking sheet.

Bake for 20 to 22 minutes. The macaroons should be slightly puffed and dry to the touch, but not hard. Allow them to cool completely on the parchment paper before removing.

Makes 18 to 20 macaroons.

1 cup coarsely chopped
   blanched almonds
1 cup sugar
1/2 cup unsweetened cocoa
   powder
1/8 teaspoon salt
2 egg whites
1/4 teaspoon almond extract

Cakes and

Tea Breads

Bab's 5th Avenue Cranberry Upside-Down Cake

The husband-and-wife restaurant team of Mark Wumkes and Barbara Prescott met while working for a multinational climate research project on the Greenland ice sheet. Mark, a contractor in Interior Alaska, found the perfect bakery partner in Barbara, a baker and cook from Jackson, Wyoming. They opened Bab's 5th Avenue Bakery in Fairbanks in January 1995, offering sandwiches and fresh baked goods such as bagels, breads, cinnamon rolls, scones, and desserts. Their darkly caramelized, orange-flavored cranberry upside-down cake deserves every rave review.

Preheat the oven to 350°F. Grease a 10-inch round or 9-inch square baking pan and line with buttered parchment paper.

Cream together the 3 tablespoons of butter and the brown sugar until crumbly. Spread the mixture in the bottom of the pan and top with the cranberries. Cream the remaining 3/4 cup butter with the granulated sugar until light and fluffy. Add the eggs and blend thoroughly. Sift together the flour, baking powder, and salt, and lightly stir into the creamed mixture. Stir in the milk, orange juice, vanilla, and zest. Do not overmix.

Pour the batter on top of the cranberries and bake 1 hour, or until the brown sugar on the bottom has caramelized and the cake tests done with a wooden toothpick. Remove to a rack to cool slightly. Run a knife around the edge of the cake while still slightly warm, and invert onto a serving platter. Let the cake cool completely before cutting.

Makes 8 to 10 servings.

3/4 cup plus 3 tablespoons butter
1 1/2 cups firmly packed dark brown sugar
3 cups cranberries
1 cup plus 2 tablespoons granulated sugar
3 eggs
2 1/4 cups all-purpose flour
1 tablespoon baking powder
3/4 teaspoon salt
1/2 cup milk
1/2 cup orange juice
3/4 teaspoon vanilla extract
Grated zest of 1 orange

Wild Blueberry Cake

*L*inda Wild, a Juneau nutritionist, got the recipe for this deceptively simple blueberry cake from her mother, Margaret Wild, who obtained it from a friend some 30 years ago. The recipe appears in many guises in Alaska cooking literature, but never more simply or better than here: a generous layer of blueberries surrounded by an exceptionally light and buttery cake. Frozen blueberries work fine for this cake—no need to defrost them first.

Preheat the oven to 350°F. Generously grease a 7-by-11-inch baking pan.

Sift together the flour, baking powder, and salt and set aside. Cream the butter with 1 cup of the sugar. Beat in the egg yolks and vanilla. Add the dry ingredients alternately with the milk, blending well after each addition; the batter will be stiff. In a separate bowl, beat the egg whites until they form soft peaks. Stir 1/4 of them into the batter, then carefully fold in the rest.

Spread half of the cake batter into the pan. Mix the berries with the remaining 2 tablespoons of sugar and sprinkle them over the batter. Top with the remaining batter and bake for about 35 minutes, until the cake tests done with a wooden toothpick. Serve warm, with a light dusting of powdered sugar and/or a mound of whipped cream.

Makes 8 servings.

1 1/2 cups all-purpose flour
1 teaspoon baking powder
1/4 teaspoon salt
1/2 cup butter
1 cup plus 2 tablespoons sugar
2 eggs, separated
1 teaspoon vanilla extract
1/3 cup milk
2 cups blueberries
Powdered sugar and/or lightly sweetened whipped cream, for serving

Lemon Pound Cake with Fresh Berries

When pie or cobbler seems too much dessert and sorbet too little, this light and lemony yogurt pound cake makes the perfect foil for Alaska's summer berries. For a richer, even more magnificent cake, use 6 eggs instead of 4 eggs.

Preheat the oven to 375°F. Grease and flour a tube or Bundt pan.

Sift together the flour, baking soda, and salt and set aside. Cream the butter until light; gradually add the sugar, and cream the mixture until light and fluffy. Beat in the eggs one at a time, then add the lemon juice. (The batter may curdle slightly but will smooth out during the next step.) Blend in the yogurt alternately with the dry ingredients, followed by the lemon zest.

Pour the batter into the prepared pan and bake for 45 minutes to 1 hour or until the cake tests done with a wooden toothpick. Cool for 10 minutes in the pan before inverting onto a rack. When completely cool, dust the cake with powdered sugar. Cut into slices and serve with the berries and a spoonful of Fresh Raspberry or Strawberry Sauce.

Makes 10 to 12 servings.

VARIATION: Instead of dusting the cake with powdered sugar, make a tart lemon glaze by stirring together 2 tablespoons lemon juice and 3/4 cup powdered sugar. Drizzle the glaze over the cooled cake.

3 cups cake flour, stirred
   before measuring
1 teaspoon baking soda
1/4 teaspoon salt
1 cup butter
2 cups sugar
4 eggs
2 tablespoons lemon juice
1 cup plain yogurt
1 tablespoon grated
   lemon zest
Powdered sugar, for dusting
About 3 cups mixed fresh
   berries, sweetened to taste,
   for serving
Fresh Raspberry or Strawberry
   Sauce (see page 95), for
   serving

Kate's Apple Snack Cake

*N*orthern bakers tend to collect apple recipes, as might be expected—any fruit that travels well, keeps beautifully, tastes wonderful raw, and can be baked into a variety of delicious goods deserves unlimited space in the recipe box. My sister, Kate, gave me this recipe for hearty, eat-out-of-your-hand apple cake. You can vary the spices to suit your mood. I often add cinnamon or cardamom. Snack cakes like this don't need to be frosted—at most, a quick dusting of powdered sugar does the job.

Preheat the oven to 350°F. Grease and flour a 9-by-13-inch baking pan.

Sift the flour, sugar, baking soda, salt, allspice, and nutmeg into a large mixing bowl. In another bowl, lightly beat the eggs, then beat in the oil and vanilla. Stir the mixture into the dry ingredients. Add the diced apples, raisins, and nuts and mix thoroughly; the batter will be very stiff. Turn the batter into the pan and bake 50 to 60 minutes or until the cake tests done with a wooden toothpick. Cool and dust with powdered sugar.

Makes 12 servings.

2 cups all-purpose flour
1 1/2 cups sugar
1 teaspoon baking soda
1/2 teaspoon salt
1 teaspoon ground allspice
1/2 teaspoon ground nutmeg
3 eggs
1 cup vegetable oil
1 teaspoon vanilla extract
4 cups peeled, diced apples
    (3 to 4 medium apples)
1 cup raisins
1 cup chopped walnuts
Powdered sugar, for dusting

Sourdough Chocolate Cake

Here is the ultimate Alaska snack cake. Made with sourdough (so each version differs slightly), this exuberant one-bowl cake fills the house with the fragrance of chocolate and bakes to a high, glossy dome. It's simple, flavorful, and substantial without being heavy, and needs no adornment. Don't be surprised if the cake forms a big crack down the center, like the crevasse of an Alaskan glacier—that's just part of its charm.

Preheat the oven to 350°F. Grease and flour a 9-by-13-inch baking pan.

Sift the flour, sugar, baking soda, salt, and cocoa powder into a large mixing bowl. Add the boiling water, sourdough starter, oil, eggs, coffee, and vanilla and beat at medium speed for 2 minutes. Pour the batter into the prepared pan and bake for 35 to 40 minutes or until the cake tests done with a wooden toothpick.

Makes 12 servings.

3 cups all-purpose flour
2 cups sugar
2 teaspoons baking soda
1/2 teaspoon salt
1/2 cup unsweetened cocoa
  powder
1 cup boiling water
1 cup Sourdough Starter
  (see page 33)
3/4 cup vegetable oil
2 eggs
2 teaspoons instant coffee
  powder
1 teaspoon vanilla extract

Spiced Buttermilk Prune Cake with Cream Cheese Icing

In Southeast Alaska, fall blows up overnight, stripping willows and salmonberries of their leaves and unleashing torrents of cold rain. Dark and fragrant with spices, this moist prune cake seems exactly the right thing to offer in this tempestuous season.

Preheat the oven to 350°F. Grease and flour two 8-inch round cake pans.

Simmer the prunes in water to cover until tender, 5 to 10 minutes. Drain and cool. Pit the prunes if necessary and chop them coarsely to obtain 2/3 cup. Resift the flour with the baking soda, salt, cinnamon, nutmeg, allspice, and cloves; set aside.

Cream the butter with the sugar until light and fluffy. Beat in the eggs one at a time, followed by the prunes. Add the dry ingredients alternately with the buttermilk, blending well after each addition, then stir in the nuts. Fill the cake pans and bake 30 to 35 minutes, until the cake tests done with a wooden toothpick. Allow to cool thoroughly before icing.

For the cream cheese icing, whip the cream cheese and butter until soft and well blended. Add the milk or cream. Gradually beat in the powdered sugar and vanilla and blend until smooth.

Makes 12 to 16 servings.

About 1 cup dried prunes
1 1/2 cups sifted all-purpose flour
1 teaspoon baking soda
1/4 teaspoon salt
1/2 teaspoon ground cinnamon
1/2 teaspoon ground nutmeg
1/2 teaspoon ground allspice
1/4 teaspoon ground cloves
1/2 cup butter
1 1/2 cups sugar
2 eggs
2/3 cup buttermilk
1/3 cup chopped walnuts

CREAM CHEESE ICING
4 ounces cream cheese
1/4 cup butter, softened
1 tablespoon milk or cream
2 cups powdered sugar
2 teaspoons vanilla extract

Applesauce Cake with Penuche Icing

This recipe for homey applesauce cake belonged to my grandmother, but transplanted well to Alaska, where hearty appetites appreciate such old-fashioned winter desserts. My grandmother made the cake using her home-canned applesauce, which she flavored heavily with cinnamon. She always finished the cake with the traditional penuche icing.

Preheat the oven to 350°F. Generously grease a tube pan.

Cream the butter with the sugar until light and fluffy. Add the eggs, beating well after each, followed by the applesauce. Sift together the flour, baking powder, baking soda, chocolate, nutmeg, cinnamon, and cloves. Stir the dry ingredients into the applesauce mixture. Stir in the raisins and nuts. Spoon the batter into the pan and bake for about 45 minutes or until the cake tests done with a toothpick. Cool in the pan for 10 minutes and then invert onto a rack. Cool completely before icing.

To make the penuche icing (essentially penuche candy or brown sugar fudge), bring the brown sugar, granulated sugar, and milk to a boil in a heavy-bottomed saucepan, stirring constantly. Then boil slowly, without stirring, until the mixture reaches the soft ball stage (238°F on a candy thermometer). Remove from the heat and mix in the butter and vanilla. Let the mixture cool to 110°F, then beat with a wooden spoon or electric mixer until the penuche turns creamy and seems about to set. Quickly pour the penuche over the cake, letting the excess flow down the sides freestyle.

Makes 10 to 12 servings.

1/2 cup butter
1 cup sugar
2 eggs
1 1/2 cups sweetened
   applesauce (15-ounce jar)
2 cups all-purpose flour
1 teaspoon baking powder
1 teaspoon baking soda
2 tablespoons sweet ground
   (powdered) chocolate
1 teaspoon ground nutmeg
1 teaspoon ground cinnamon
1 teaspoon ground cloves
1 cup raisins
1 cup chopped walnuts

PENUCHE ICING
3 cups firmly packed brown
   sugar
1 cup granulated sugar
1 cup milk
2 tablespoons butter
1 teaspoon vanilla extract

Tangerine Cheesecake

etsy Brenneman, a familiar face and voice to viewers of Juneau's public television station, KTOO-TV (sent in that pledge yet?), collects cheesecake recipes in real life. Bless her. This one produces a luscious, rich—well, downright sensuous—cheesecake that captures the distinctive flavor of tangerines. Definitely a celebration cake.

Preheat the oven to 400°F.

For the crust, stir together the flour, sugar, and tangerine zest. Cut in the butter until the mixture resembles coarse meal. Add the egg yolk and vanilla and mix to form a dough, kneading until smooth. Pat one third of the dough onto the bottom of a 9-inch springform pan and bake for 5 minutes or until golden. Remove from the oven and reduce the temperature to 350°F for baking the cheesecake. When the bottom crust has cooled, pat the remaining dough around the sides of the pan to within 1/2 inch of the top. Set aside while you make the filling.

Using an electric mixer, beat the cream cheese at low speed until smooth and creamy. Sift or stir together the sugar, flour, and salt. Gradually add the flour mixture to the cream cheese, beating at low speed. Beat in the eggs and egg yolks, one at a time, followed by the tangerine juice, zest, and vanilla. Pour the filling into the crust and bake for 45 minutes to 1 hour. The cheesecake should be golden, and set around the perimeter but still moist in the center. Let the cheesecake stand in the turned-off oven with the door ajar. When completely cool, transfer to the refrigerator to chill thoroughly before serving.

Makes 10 to 12 servings.

CRUST
1 cup all-purpose flour
1/4 cup sugar
1 tablespoon grated
 tangerine zest
1/2 cup cold butter
1 egg yolk
1/2 teaspoon vanilla extract

FILLING
5 packages (8 ounces each)
 cream cheese, at room
 temperature
1 3/4 cups sugar
3 tablespoons all-purpose flour
1/4 teaspoon salt
5 whole eggs
2 egg yolks
1/2 cup tangerine juice
 (3 to 4 tangerines)
1 tablespoon grated
 tangerine zest
1/4 teaspoon vanilla extract

Chocolate Almond Torte with Raspberry Sauce

*W*inter is Alaska's social season. With shortened days curtailing outdoor activities, the focus shifts inward, to holiday parties and leisurely dinners catching up with friends. This elegant torte, with a moist, fudge-textured center and glossy, dark chocolate glaze, escapes being too rich or too sweet and makes a fine close to a fancy meal.

Preheat the oven to 350°F. Grease an 8-inch round cake pan and dust with cocoa powder or flour.

Melt the chocolate with the coffee over low heat or in a microwave, and set aside to cool. Cream the butter with the sugar until light, and add the egg yolks, blending well. Stir in the chocolate, flour, and ground almonds.

Whip the egg whites with the salt until soft peaks form. Stir a spoonful into the chocolate mixture to lighten the batter, then fold in the remaining egg whites and spread the batter in the prepared pan. Bake the torte 25 to 30 minutes—no longer! The cake should look dry on top and slightly puffed, and show a faint separation from the pan. A toothpick inserted near the rim of the cake should emerge dry but show moist crumbs in the center. Let the cake rest on a rack a few minutes before turning out of the pan, and cool completely before glazing.

For the glaze, melt the chocolate in a small pan over low heat or in a microwave. Remove from the heat and stir in the butter, making sure each piece dissolves before adding the next. Stir in the almond extract or Amaretto. Let the glaze cool, stirring frequently—it will thicken slightly as it cools—and then apply it quickly to the top and sides of the cooled torte. Serve in small wedges with lightly sweetened whipped cream or Crème Fraîche and a spoonful of Fresh Raspberry Sauce.

Makes 8 to 10 servings.

Unsweetened cocoa powder
  or flour for dusting pan
4 ounces (4 squares)
  semisweet baking chocolate
2 tablespoons strong coffee
1/2 cup butter
3/4 cup sugar
3 eggs, separated
1/2 cup cake flour, stirred
  before measuring
1/3 cup finely ground blanched
  almonds
1/8 teaspoon salt
Whipped cream or Crème
  Fraîche (see page 47)
Raspberry Sauce
  (see page 95)

CHOCOLATE GLAZE
2 ounces (2 squares)
  semisweet baking chocolate
2 tablespoons butter, cut in
  small pieces
1/4 teaspoon almond extract
  or 1 tablespoon Amaretto

Crème Fraîche

To make crème fraîche, a French-style cultured cream, heat to luke warm 1 cup heavy cream mixed with 1 teaspoon commercial buttermilk. Transfer the mixture to a glass jar and leave at room temperature until thickened, usually 1 to 2 days. Use plain or whipped, with or without sweetening. Once cultured, crème fraîche keeps in the refrigerator for a week or more.

Two Sisters Blitz Torte

Carri Thurman was a 20-year-old ski bum looking for a place to light when she took a job in a hotel restaurant on 5-mile-long Homer Spit. Eight years later she opened the Two Sisters Bakery, a small, downhome kind of place located in an old Homer building. She can see the mountains and water from her baking table. Carri's German grandmother made this memorable Blitz Torte for family birthdays and reunions. Carri and her sister resurrected the recipe, and the Blitz Torte became a signature dessert.

Imagine two layers, each consisting of a yellow cake base, a baked-on meringue, and a crusty topping of cinnamon, sugar, and nuts. Between the two layers floats a wonderfully gooey custard filling. True comfort food! The torte makes a beautiful and unusual presentation and needs no icing or other adornment. Evaporated milk gives the custard cream a distinctive caramel color and flavor in this recipe. Substitute fresh cream or milk if you wish.

Preheat the oven to 350°F. Line two 8-inch round baking pans with parchment paper and grease lightly.

Cream the butter. Gradually add the sugar and beat the mixture until light and fluffy. Blend in the egg yolks one at a time, then add the vanilla. Sift together the flour, baking powder, and salt, and add to the batter alternately with the buttermilk. Divide the batter between the 2 pans and spread evenly. The batter will just cover the bottom of each pan. Set the pans aside while you proceed with the meringue layer.

Beat the egg whites until frothy. Add the cream of tartar and continue beating on high speed until soft peaks form. Reduce the speed to medium and gradually add the sugar. Return to high speed and continue beating until the meringue holds glossy peaks that are fairly stiff but not dry. Spread the meringue over the cake batter in each pan. Combine the almonds, sugar, and cinnamon and distribute over the meringue. Place the pans in the oven and bake 30 minutes.

1/2 cup butter
1/2 cup sugar
4 egg yolks
1 teaspoon vanilla extract
1 cup flour
1 teaspoon baking powder
1/4 teaspoon salt
3 tablespoons buttermilk

MERINGUE LAYER
4 egg whites
1/4 teaspoon cream of tartar
3/4 cup sugar
1/2 cup sliced almonds
1 tablespoon sugar
1/2 teaspoon cinnamon

The meringues should be brown and crusty on top, and a toothpick inserted into the bottom cake layer should come out dry. Let the cakes cool in the pans on racks.

To make the custard cream, scald the milk with 1/4 cup of the sugar. Meanwhile, beat the egg yolks with a whisk or electric beater. Gradually blend in the remaining 1/2 cup sugar, the cornstarch, and the vanilla. Beating continuously, dribble the hot milk mixture into the egg yolks. Return the mixture to the pan and cook over moderate heat, stirring continuously, until the custard thickens and comes to a boil. It will be quite thick. Remove from the heat and whisk out any lumps. Transfer the custard to a glass bowl and cool slightly, then smooth a layer of plastic wrap directly on the surface of the custard and chill.

To assemble the Blitz Torte, run a knife around the inside of the pans. Insert a spatula beneath one of the cake layers, lift from the pan, and place on a serving platter, discarding the parchment paper (keep the cake meringue side up–do not invert). Spread the custard cream on top. Unmold the second cake layer and place on top of the custard cream. Serve immediately or refrigerate.

Makes 8 servings.

CUSTARD CREAM FILLING
2 cups evaporated milk
3/4 cup sugar
4 egg yolks
3 tablespoons cornstarch
1 teaspoon vanilla extract

Gingerbread

*F*or several years while we lived in Juneau, the first snow of the season fell on Halloween, dusting the costumes of the trick-or-treaters as they made their rounds up and down the staircases of Starr Hill. After placing a jack-o'-lantern in the window to signal our presence, we would settle in front of the fireplace with hot cider and gingerbread, listening for the footfalls of little ghosts and goblins.

My mother served this dark, glossy gingerbread as a winter dessert throughout my childhood. The recipe evidently made the rounds of several church cookbooks, including *Ketchikan Kookery,* a small volume published in 1912 by the Ladies Aid of the Methodist Episcopal Church. Some Alaskans add blueberries to their gingerbread and serve it with lemon sauce. I like mine with whipped cream or butter.

Preheat the oven to 350°F. Grease and flour a 9-by-13-inch baking pan.

Sift the flour with the ginger, cinnamon, and cloves and set aside. Cream the butter and sugar until light and fluffy, then beat in the egg, followed by the molasses. Dissolve the baking soda in the boiling water and add to the molasses mixture alternately with the dry ingredients. Mix well and pour the batter into the prepared pan. Bake for 30 minutes or until the gingerbread tests done with a wooden toothpick. Cut into squares and serve warm with softened butter or whipped cream.

Makes 8 to 10 servings.

1 1/4 cups all-purpose flour
1/2 teaspoon ground ginger
1/2 teaspoon ground cinnamon
1/2 teaspoon ground cloves
1/4 cup butter
1/4 cup sugar
1 egg
1/2 cup molasses
1 teaspoon baking soda
1/2 cup boiling water
Softened butter or whipped cream, for serving

Rie's Dutch Honey Cake

During her childhood, artist Rie Muñoz, our Juneau neighbor, traveled with her family regularly between the United States and Holland, her parents' homeland. In Holland they looked forward to this traditional honey-flavored breakfast cake, usually accompanied by some good Gouda or Edam cheese. Now in her 70s, Rie devotes most of her travels to sketching remote villages in Alaska or France. She often bakes miniature loaves of this cake to distribute to friends at Christmas. Gently spiced and not overly sweet, the cake can be eaten alone or with cheese, or toasted and slathered with butter and marmalade.

This recipe contains no eggs and no cooking oil or other fat. That and the 181 steps Rie climbs to her house each day may account for her excellent fitness and the 50 to 60 paintings she manages to produce each year.

Preheat the oven to 300°F. Grease 2 standard loaf pans.

Mix together the flour, sugar, baking soda, salt, cinnamon, allspice, nutmeg, cloves, and lemon zest. In another bowl, stir together the buttermilk and honey, and add to the dry ingredients. Stir lightly, adding buttermilk as needed for a moist batter. Divide between the prepared pans and bake 1 hour or until the cakes test done with a wooden toothpick. Allow to cool before slicing.

Makes 2 loaves.

4 cups all-purpose flour
2 cups sugar
1 teaspoon baking soda
Pinch of salt
1 teaspoon ground cinnamon
1 teaspoon ground allspice
1/2 teaspoon ground nutmeg
1/4 teaspoon ground cloves
1/2 teaspoon grated
    lemon zest
1 3/4 cups buttermilk, more
    if needed
5 tablespoons honey

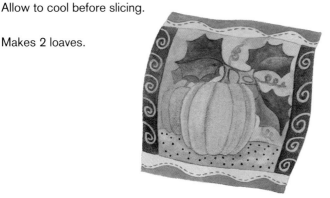

Tenakee Orange Pecan Bread

*A*t least once a summer we try to get out to Tenakee Springs, a community of about 100 full-time residents on the east side of Chichagof Island, a ferry or floatplane ride from Juneau. Favored with hot sulfur springs and plentiful Dungeness crab, Tenakee developed early on into an offbeat R&R center—a place with one street (a footpath, really), no vehicles, and limited indoor plumbing. People come here to kick back and relax: soak in the hot spring, take walks, pick berries, read books, catch crab, and visit with friends. We generally end up cooking and eating a lot.

The recipe for this sturdy, pecan-studded loaf comes from Elsie Pegues, whose family owns and operates the Tenakee general store and rental cabins, and appears in Tasty Treats from Tenakee Springs, Alaska. Redolent with molasses and orange, the bread becomes more flavorful and aromatic with each passing day, so there's much to be said for baking at least a day in advance. I like this bread sliced thinly and spread with cream cheese flavored with a bit of orange zest.

Preheat the oven to 350°F. Grease and flour 2 loaf pans.

Sift the all-purpose flour, sugar, baking powder, and salt into a large mixing bowl. Stir in the whole wheat flour, pecans, and orange zest. In another bowl, beat the egg, then add the milk, molasses, orange juice, and vanilla, blending well. Stir in the melted butter.

Make a well in the dry ingredients and add the liquid mixture all at once. Stir gently with a fork, just enough to combine the wet and dry ingredients. Divide the batter between the pans and bake for about 1 hour or until the breads test done with a wooden toothpick. Cool slightly in the pans before removing to a rack. Cool thoroughly before slicing.

Makes 2 loaves.

2 cups sifted all-purpose flour
3/4 cup sugar
4 teaspoons baking powder
1/2 teaspoon salt
1 cup unsifted whole
   wheat flour
1 1/2 cups coarsely
   chopped pecans
Grated zest of 1 orange
1 egg
1/2 cup milk
1/2 cup molasses
1/2 cup orange juice
1 1/2 teaspoons vanilla extract
5 tablespoons butter, melted
   and slightly cooled

Apricot Almond Loaf

One ne gold rush guide recommended that miners and prospectors en route to the Klondike *include 20 pounds of dried apricots in their year's worth of supplies (also 10 pounds of dried peaches and 25 pounds each of dried apples and prunes). While I don't keep quite that quantity on hand, I do find them delicious and useful in many recipes, from cookies to granola. With almonds they form one of those magical taste combinations, like raspberries and chocolate.*

Preheat the oven to 350°F. Lightly grease and flour a standard loaf pan.

Sift the flour, sugar, baking powder, and salt into a mixing bowl. Mix in the almonds and apricots and set aside. In another bowl, lightly beat the egg. Blend in the milk and oil, and add the mixture to the dry ingredients, stirring lightly. Bake 50 to 60 minutes, until the bread tests done with a wooden toothpick.

Makes 1 loaf.

2 cups all-purpose flour
3/4 cup sugar
1 tablespoon baking powder
1/2 teaspoon salt
1 cup finely chopped
  blanched almonds
3/4 cup coarsely chopped
  dried apricots
1 egg
1 cup milk
1/4 cup vegetable oil

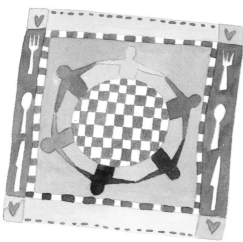

Kitty's Cranberry Orange Bread

*F*all colors the Interior like nowhere else in Alaska, splashing the tundra with hues of cranberry and orange. Kitty Mathers bakes the same combination into this fall loaf, using low-bush cranberries that she gathers from a hill near her Fairbanks home. She picks them after the first frost, for maximum sweetness. Cultivated cranberries may be substituted.

Preheat the oven to 350°F. Grease a standard loaf pan.

Sift or stir together the flour, sugar, baking powder, baking soda, and salt and set aside. In another bowl, blend the orange juice, egg, oil or butter, and orange zest. Lightly stir this mixture into the dry ingredients and fold in the cranberries.

Spoon the batter into the loaf pan and bake about 1 hour or until a wooden toothpick comes out clean. Allow the bread to cool thoroughly before slicing.

Makes 1 loaf.

2 cups all-purpose flour
1 cup sugar
1/2 teaspoon baking powder
1/2 teaspoon baking soda
1/2 teaspoon salt
3/4 cup orange juice
1 egg, lightly beaten
2 tablespoons vegetable oil or
   melted butter
Grated zest of 1 orange
1 cup cranberries, whole or
   coarsely chopped

Gustavus Inn Grasshopper Pie

When my husband and I first visited the Gustavus Inn in 1969, we found ourselves drawn into the busy lives of Jack and Sally Lesh and their eight children. The family worked hard to carve out a living in this gateway community to Glacier Bay. Jack kept the equipment functioning and cultivated an enormous vegetable garden. Sally drove the school bus and operated the weather station and the community telephone. Meanwhile, the inn gained a reputation for the best home cooking in Alaska. Operated now by Jack and Sally's son David and his wife, JoAnn, the homestead still offers the genuine warmth of Alaskan hospitality, along with sumptuous meals of local seafood and freshly baked breads and pastries. This Grasshopper Pie, conveniently served from the freezer, remains a Gustavus Inn fixture.

Preheat the oven to 350°F.

For the crust, combine the chocolate wafer crumbs and sugar in a mixing bowl. Stir in the melted butter and press the mixture onto the bottom and sides of an 8-inch pie pan. Bake 8 minutes and set aside to cool.

Place the marshmallows and milk in the top of a double boiler and stir over simmering water until the marshmallows melt completely; set aside. When nearly cool, thoroughly mix in the crème de menthe and crème de cacao. Fold in the whipped cream and pour the filling into the prepared crust. Place the pie in the freezer, covering the surface with plastic wrap when completely frozen. Remove from the freezer a few minutes before serving.

Makes 8 servings.

BRANDY ALEXANDER VARIATION: Melt 2 ounces unsweetened chocolate with the marshmallows and milk, and substitute brandy for the crème de menthe.

CRUST
1 1/4 cups finely crushed
  chocolate wafers
1 tablespoon sugar
3 tablespoons melted butter

FILLING
1/2 pound white
  marshmallows
1/4 cup milk
3 tablespoons green crème
  de menthe
2 tablespoons clear crème
  de cacao
1 cup heavy cream, whipped

Crondahls' Fresh Berry Pie

The entrance to Jay and Judy Crondahl's bed-and-breakfast leads off the midway point of the Fifth Street Stairs in downtown Juneau (49 steps down to East Street; 46 steps up to Kennedy Street). More often than not, the house bulges with a lively assortment of neighbors and friends, children, grandchildren, bed-and-breakfast guests, and passersby on the stairs pausing to catch their breath. It is a truly happy gathering when Jay and Judy produce one of their fresh berry pies.

Raspberries, blueberries, and strawberries all work beautifully in this classic recipe. Or use a combination, with a few thimbleberries or nagoonberries thrown in for good measure. When Jay, an enthusiastic canoeist, goes camping in berry country, he takes along a prepared pie shell, premeasured sugar and cornstarch, and canned whipping cream, and creates this pie with whatever berries he finds.

1 prebaked 9-inch pie shell
  (see page 64)
3/4 cup sugar
2 1/2 tablespoons cornstarch
1 cup water
4 cups fresh berries
Whipped cream, for serving

Combine the sugar and cornstarch in a heavy-bottomed saucepan. Add the water and cook over moderate heat, stirring, until thickened. Remove from the heat. Puree or crush 1 cup of the berries and stir them into the cornstarch mixture. Arrange the remaining berries in the pie shell and pour the crushed berry mixture on top. Chill the pie thoroughly to set, and serve with whipped cream.

Makes 8 servings.

Lemon Meringue Pie

If you want to delight your Alaskan friends, pack a basket of large, juicy lemons when you board the plane from the Lower 48. (Avocados and peaches also score highly as hostess gifts.) Lemons often cost so much in Alaska that most cooks learn to substitute bottled or frozen lemon juice to good effect. But this tart pie, clamored for on family birthdays, deserves the real thing.

For the filling, mix the sugar, flour, and cornstarch in a heavy-bottomed saucepan. Add the water and cook over medium heat, stirring, until the mixture thickens and turns clear. Whisk in the egg yolks, lemon juice, lemon zest, and butter. Return the pan to medium-low heat and cook the filling until thick, stirring constantly and taking care the mixture does not scorch. Taste, adding lemon juice as needed to achieve the desired tartness. Let the filling cool slightly and then strain into the prepared pie shell. Cool thoroughly before proceeding with the meringue.

Preheat the oven to 350°F.

For the meringue, beat the egg whites until frothy. Add the vanilla and cream of tartar and continue beating on high speed until soft peaks form. Reduce the speed to medium and beat in the sugar a spoonful or two at a time. Return to high speed and continue beating until the egg whites are glossy and fairly stiff but not dry. Pile the meringue on the filling, completely covering the edge of the crust.

Bake for 15 minutes, until golden. Cool completely before serving, but do not refrigerate.

Makes 8 servings.

1 prebaked 9-inch pie shell
(see page 64)

FILLING
1 1/2 cups sugar
6 tablespoons all-purpose flour
6 tablespoons cornstarch
2 1/4 cups water
6 egg yolks
1/2 cup lemon juice, more to
taste
1 tablespoon grated lemon
zest
1 tablespoon butter

MERINGUE (see note, page 59)
6 egg whites
1 teaspoon vanilla extract
1/4 teaspoon cream of tartar
3/4 cup powdered sugar

Red Currant and Almond Pie

*R*ed currants thrive throughout Alaska, excepting the extremes of the Arctic, the Aleutian Islands, and the southern Panhandle. From Mary Bishop of Fairbanks comes this delectable pie, enjoyed when the prized red currants ripen in late July or August.

Preheat the oven to 450°F.

Line a 9-inch pie pan with half of the pastry, and sprinkle with the chopped almonds. Stir together the currants, sugar, flour, and almond extract and spoon the filling into the shell. Cover with a lattice top made from the remaining pastry, and crimp the edges. Bake the pie for 10 minutes. Reduce the temperature to 350°F and bake 30 minutes longer or until bubbling. Serve hot or cold.

Makes 8 servings.

Pastry for a 9-inch double
  crust pie (see pages 64-65)
2/3 cup blanched almonds,
  finely chopped
4 cups red currants
2 cups sugar
1/2 cup all-purpose flour
1/2 teaspoon almond extract

◄ A Cautionary Note Due to the possible presence of harmful salmonella bacteria in raw or undercooked eggs, USDA safety guidelines specify cooking eggs to an internal temperature of 160°F and baking a meringue for 15 minutes at 350°F. However, you should always consider yourself at risk when consuming such foods. Very high-risk individuals, including children, the elderly, and those suffering from immune-deficiency disorders, should probably avoid them altogether.

Riversong Lodge Blueberry–Cranberry Pie

In 1983 Kirsten Dixon, a public health nurse, and Carl Dixon, an audiologist turned fishing guide, built a log lodge on the Yentna River in the wilderness northwest of Anchorage. When their large black cookstoves finally arrived by floatplane, they hauled them up the riverbank by hand. With no prior experience operating a lodge or a commercial kitchen, or even living in the bush, they created Riversong Lodge, nurturing two small daughters in the process.

Visitors come to Riversong from all over the world. Kirsten, now a veteran of cooking classes at the Paris Cordon Bleu and Boston University, presides over a kitchen that produces miraculous dishes from the bounty of her greenhouse, garden, and surrounding woods. This "winter pie" takes advantage of the cache of berries stored in most Alaskans' freezers. You can bake the pie successfully without thawing the berries first, but the cooking time must be increased by 10 to 15 minutes.

Preheat the oven to 400°F.

Place the blueberries and cranberries in a large bowl. Combine the sugar, tapioca, and salt and stir the mixture into the berries. Line a 9-inch pie pan with half the pastry. Spoon the filling into the pastry and dot with the butter. Top with the remaining pastry, crimp the edges, and slash the top in several places to allow the steam to escape. Lightly brush the crust with cold water.

Bake on the center rack of the oven for 45 to 50 minutes, until the crust browns and juice bubbles consistently from the vents.

Makes 8 servings.

Pastry for a 9-inch double-crust pie (see pages 64-65)
2 cups blueberries
2 cups cranberries
1 cup sugar
3 tablespoons quick-cooking tapioca
Pinch of salt
2 tablespoons butter

Turner Lake Pecan Pie

One summer weekend we rented the Forest Service recreational cabin at West Turner Lake, arguably the most beautiful of the more than 170 wilderness cabins in the Tongass National Forest that the federal government makes available to the public at nominal expense. Our friends Bob and Lee Grogan—experienced outdoorspeople, unlike ourselves—came too. After dinner the first evening, Lee rummaged around in one of the boxes that had made the floatplane ride with us from Juneau. Like a conjurer, she brought out a beautiful pecan pie, which we enjoyed while watching the sky and water merge into one. Ah, wilderness!

Preheat the oven to 350°F.

Cream the butter with the brown sugar. Blend in the eggs, then the corn syrup and vanilla. Pour the filling into the pie shell and arrange the nuts on top. Bake until a knife inserted in the center of the pie comes out clean, 45 minutes to 1 hour. Serve alone or accompany with whipped cream or vanilla ice cream.

Makes 8 servings.

1 unbaked 9-inch pie shell (see page 64)
2 tablespoons softened butter
1/2 cup firmly packed brown sugar
3 eggs, lightly beaten
1 cup light corn syrup
1 teaspoon vanilla extract
1 1/2 cups pecans, chopped or halves
Whipped cream or vanilla ice cream, for serving (optional)

Lisianski Inlet Rhubarb Pie

*G*ail Corbin, the magistrate at Pelican, a cannery village on the northwest corner of Chichagof Island, began homesteading her property on Lisianski Inlet in 1968. Today she operates the homestead as a small, informal summer wilderness lodge where visitors get a taste of the "real Alaska." Humpback whales cruise past the living room window, brown bears amble out of the woods. Gail leads berry-picking expeditions and excursions to look at sea otters and birds. But I just enjoy watching her deal with the challenges of operating a wilderness homestead: keeping the generator going, tending the garden, maintaining the skiffs, baking the pies.

Gail bakes rhubarb pie in spring when this first fruit of the season rears its welcome head in the garden. When blueberries and salmonberries ripen in July, she mixes them with rhubarb to make her summer pies.

Preheat the oven to 425°F.

Line a 9- or 10-inch pie pan with half of the pastry and fill with the diced rhubarb. Beat the eggs until foamy and light. Add the sugar, flour, salt, and optional nutmeg, and blend well. Pour the mixture over the rhubarb. Cover with the top crust, crimp the edges, and slash in several places to allow the steam to escape.

Bake the pie for 10 minutes, then reduce the temperature to 350°F and bake for 45 minutes longer.

Makes 8 servings.

Pastry for a 9- or 10-inch double crust pie (see pages 64-65)
5 cups finely diced rhubarb
2 eggs
1 1/2 cups sugar
3 tablespoons all-purpose flour
1/4 teaspoon salt
1/4 teaspoon ground nutmeg (optional)

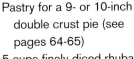

Robbie Jayne Johnson's Grand Champion Coventry Cream Cheese Tartlets

*R*obbie Jayne Johnson of Anchorage has been entering crafts, sewing, jams, jellies, breads, and desserts in the Alaska State Fair at Palmer for 24 years. Occasionally she gets carried away. In 1996, for example, she created 170 entries (and won 125 ribbons). Her Coventry Cream Cheese Tartlets took the Grand Champion award one August and account for at least 12 blue ribbons from other competitions. She uses tartlet pans of several different shapes, including round, oblong, diamond, and heart.

Line 24 tartlet pans (2 to 3 inches long by about 3/4 inch deep) with pastry and prick all over with a fork. Chill while preparing the filling.

Preheat the oven to 450°F.

Blend the cream cheese with the butter until light and fluffy. Blend in the sugar, egg yolks, orange juice, salt, and nutmeg. Fill the tartlets to within 1/8 inch of the rim, place them on ungreased baking sheets, and bake for 10 minutes. Reduce the oven temperature to 325°F and bake 15 minutes longer, or until brown and firm.

Invert the tartlets onto a sheet of waxed paper, removing the pans. When cool, turn them right side up and spread with apricot preserves (about 1/2 tablespoon per tart). Serve the same day.

Makes 24 tartlets.

Pastry for a 9-inch double-crust pie (see pages 64-65)
8 ounces cream cheese, softened
1/4 cup butter, softened
1/2 cup sugar
2 egg yolks
1 tablespoon orange juice
1/2 teaspoon salt
1/4 teaspoon ground nutmeg
About 2/3 cup apricot preserves

PIE CRUSTS

*Choose one of these three crusts for each of the pie recipes in this book,
or use your own favorite pastry dough. The key to making tender, flaky pie crust—
whether with lard, shortening, butter, or a combination of fats—is to use the absolute
minimum of water and handle the dough as little as possible. Be sure to "cut,"
not stir, the fat into the flour. If time allows, chill the dough for about
30 minutes before rolling and shaping.*

Rich Pie Crust

*This basic recipe produces a very short, all-purpose crust. Substituting butter for half
the shortening adds color and flavor and results in a slightly firmer crust.*

Sift the flour, sugar, and salt into a mixing bowl. Cut in the shortening with a pastry blender, two knives, or your fingertips until the mixture resembles very coarse meal. Sprinkle the water over the mixture a tablespoon at a time, stirring and lifting lightly with a fork, until the dough just holds together when pressed in your hand. Gather the mass into a rough ball and transfer to the refrigerator or to a floured board for rolling.

2 cups all-purpose flour
1 tablespoon sugar
1/2 teaspoon salt
1 cup vegetable shortening
  (or 1/2 cup shortening plus
  1/2 cup chilled butter)
4 to 5 tablespoons very
  cold water

Makes two 9-inch crusts.

PREBAKED PIE SHELL: Prepare selected pastry as directed. Roll out half the dough and fit into a 9-inch or smaller pie pan. Trim the pastry to 1/2 to 1 inch beyond the rim, fold, and crimp in a decorative pattern. Pierce the bottom and sides of the pastry with a fork. Repeat with the second portion of the dough. Chill the shells before baking in a preheated 400°F oven for 10 to 12 minutes until golden. Cool before filling. Makes two 9-inch shells.

Food Processor Sour Cream Crust

Although not quite as flaky as a traditional short crust, this foolproof pastry looks pretty, tastes delicious, and handles like a dream.

Place the flour, sugar, salt, butter, and shortening in the bowl of a food processor and pulse until crumbly. Add the sour cream and cold water. Pulse once or twice to blend the ingredients, scrape down the sides of the bowl, and process just until a dough forms. (Do not overprocess or dough will be tough.) Chill briefly, and roll out on a floured board.

Makes two 9-inch crusts.

2 1/2 cups all-purpose flour
1 teaspoon sugar
1/2 teaspoon salt
1/2 cup butter, chilled
1/2 cup vegetable shortening
6 tablespoons sour cream
2 tablespoons very cold water

Whole Wheat Crust

Many Alaskan home bakers prefer the more robust flavor and texture of a combination whole wheat and white flour crust. I especially like this crust for juicy berry pies.

Sift the all-purpose flour, sugar, and salt into a mixing bowl. Stir in the whole wheat flour. Cut in the shortening with a pastry blender, two knives, or your fingertips until the mixture resembles very coarse meal. Sprinkle the water over the mixture a tablespoon at a time, stirring and lifting lightly with a fork, until the dough holds together when pressed in your hand. Gather into a rough ball and chill or roll out on a floured board.

Makes two 9-inch crusts.

1 cup all-purpose flour
1 tablespoon sugar
1/2 teaspoon salt
1 cup whole wheat flour
3/4 cup vegetable shortening
3 to 4 tablespoons very cold water

Double Musky Chocolate Pie

*B*aked at the legendary Double Musky Inn in Girdwood, near Mount Alyeska, this *strange and wonderful dark chocolate concoction may be the most famous pie in Alaska.*

Preheat the oven to 350°F. Grease a 9-inch pie pan.

For the crust, beat the egg whites with the cream of tartar and salt until they form soft peaks. Gradually add the sugar, beating continually, until the whites are stiff and glossy but not dry. Fold in the pecans, cracker crumbs, and vanilla, making sure the crackers are evenly distributed and coated with meringue. Spread into the prepared pan, and smooth to a thickness of 1 inch. Bake the crust until lightly browned around the edges, about 12 minutes. Cool slightly. Leave the oven set to 350°F.

For the filling, melt the butter and chocolate together in the top of a double boiler. Add the eggs, 1/2 cup of the sugar, and 2 tablespoons of the flour, and stir briefly (less than half a minute). Add the remaining sugar and flour, stirring just until combined. (The filling will be granular.)

Pour the filling into the crust and bake for 35 minutes. The pie will be slightly crusty on top but moist in the center— a toothpick will *not* come out clean. Refrigerate, and serve with whipped cream or vanilla ice cream.

Makes 8 servings.

CRUST

3 egg whites, at room temperature
1/4 teaspoon cream of tartar
Pinch of salt
1 cup sugar
1 cup pecans, coarsely chopped
36 2-inch saltine crackers, broken into 1/2-inch pieces
1 tablespoon vanilla extract

FILLING

1/2 cup butter
2 ounces (2 squares) unsweetened baking chocolate
2 eggs
1 cup sugar
1/4 cup all-purpose flour
Whipped cream or vanilla ice cream, for serving

Hälsingland Hotel Peanut Butter Cream Pie

In 1903 the U.S. Army constructed Fort William H. Seward on a lovely cove framed by the raw peaks of the Chilkat Mountains, near the present town of Haines. Now a national historic site, the white-pillared buildings ringing the parade green—one of the most arresting images in Alaska—house private residences and businesses and a nonprofit Indian arts workshop. The former bachelor officers' quarters, captains' quarters, and commanding officers' quarters form part of the Hälsingland Hotel and Commander's Room Restaurant. While seafood, especially crab, gets star billing at the restaurant, locals go for this Peanut Butter Cream Pie created by Hälsingland chef David Pruett.

Preheat the oven to 350°F.

For the crust, combine the graham cracker crumbs, pecans, and powdered sugar. Add the melted butter and stir to combine. Press the mixture onto the bottom and sides of a 9-inch pie pan, and bake for 8 minutes or until lightly browned. Allow to cool thoroughly before proceeding with the filling.

Place the peanut butter in the warmed bowl of an electric mixer. Starting on low speed, gradually beat in the powdered sugar, followed by 1/2 cup of the cream, while slowly increasing the speed to high. This will lighten the mixture for the next step. In another bowl, whip the remaining 1/2 cup cream to soft peaks, and fold the whipped cream into the peanut butter mixture. Transfer the filling to the prepared crust and smooth the top.

For the topping, whip the cream with the sugar and orange zest to form firm peaks. Mound or pipe the whipped cream on top of the filling, taking care not to cover the crust. Garnish with peanuts and chocolate, and chill thoroughly before serving.

Makes 8 to 10 servings.

CRUST

1 cup graham cracker crumbs
1/2 cup finely ground pecans
1 tablespoon powdered sugar
1/4 cup butter, melted

FILLING

2 cups unsweetened crunchy
   peanut butter, at room
   temperature
2 tablespoons powdered sugar
1 cup heavy cream

TOPPING

1 cup heavy cream
2 tablespoons powdered sugar
1 tablespoon grated orange
   zest
Chopped dry-roasted peanuts
   and shaved semisweet
   chocolate, for garnish

Peter Fitzmaurice's Tennessee Chess Pie

*P*eter Fitzmaurice, chief ranger for Kenai Fjords National Park—a 600,000-acre naturalist's laboratory of glaciers, fjords, islands, whales, sea lions, and nesting puffins encompassing most of the Harding Icefield—lives in Seward with his wife, Shannon, and their baby son. Most years, they join a gang of friends at Thanksgiving or Christmas, or both, for the traditional turkey feast, highlighted by homemade pies of all persuasions. Peter contributes this Tennessee Chess Pie, a powerful concoction whose ingredients he attempts to conceal from his health-conscious friends (at least until they've given favorable reviews). The recipe came from a redheaded former classmate at Stanford University whose granny, said to be the recipe's originator, hailed from Tennessee. Serve small *slices of this pie.*

For the crust, combine the graham cracker crumbs, powdered sugar, and optional cinnamon. Add the melted butter and stir to combine. Press the mixture into a 9-inch pie pan and chill at least 1 hour before adding the filling.

Preheat the oven to 250°F.

Beat the egg yolks until thick and foamy, and set aside. Place the sticks of butter (leave them whole) in a medium saucepan with the sugar. Cook over medium heat, stirring, until the butter melts and combines with the sugar. Gradually whisk this mixture into the egg yolks, followed by the vanilla and nutmeg.

Pour into the crust and bake for about 90 minutes. The filling will thicken into a firm, almost translucent custard with a thin meringue-like crust on top. A knife inserted into the filling should come out clean. Allow to cool thoroughly before serving.

Makes 8 to 10 servings.

CRUST
1 1/2 cups graham cracker crumbs (crackers from 1 pack of a 3-pack, or 1-pound, box)
1/4 cup powdered sugar
1 teaspoon ground cinnamon (optional)
6 tablespoons butter, melted

FILLING
6 egg yolks
1 cup butter
1 cup sugar
1/2 teaspoon vanilla extract
1/4 teaspoon ground nutmeg

Blueberry Raspberry Cobbler

For those who love baking, the glory of Alaska's summers lies in the variety of wild berries rewarding those with nimble fingers and a two-pound coffee can. The combination of blueberries and raspberries produces a beautifully colored cobbler with an intense berry flavor. If you like lots of unadulterated berry juice beneath your biscuit topping, leave out the cornstarch, which thickens the juice very slightly.

For the biscuit topping, combine the flour, sugar, baking powder, and salt. Cut in the shortening until the mixture resembles coarse meal, then add the milk and mix gently with a fork. Gather the dough into a rough ball and knead a couple of turns to smooth. Chill until ready to roll out.

Preheat the oven to 400°F.

Combine the blueberries, raspberries, sugar, and optional cornstarch in an 8-inch square pan, deep-dish pie pan, or casserole. Place in the oven until the fruit bubbles around the edges of the pan.

While the fruit heats, pat or roll the biscuit dough to a thickness of 3/8 inch. Cut into rounds or squares and arrange them on top of the hot berries. Sprinkle generously with sugar and return the cobbler to the oven and bake until golden, about 15 minutes. Serve warm, with heavy cream or vanilla ice cream.

Makes 6 servings.

BISCUIT TOPPING

2 cups all-purpose flour
2 tablespoons sugar, plus
    more to sprinkle on top
2 teaspoons baking powder
1 teaspoon salt
6 tablespoons vegetable
    shortening (or 3 tablespoons
    shortening plus 3 tablespoons
    butter, for additional flavor)
3/4 cup milk

FILLING

4 cups blueberries
2 cups raspberries
1/2 cup sugar
1 tablespoon cornstarch
    (optional)
Heavy cream or vanilla ice
    cream, for serving

Strawberry Shortcake

*O*nce, while riding the Alaska ferry, I sat near two men discussing the unlikely topic of strawberry shortcake. They were decrying the hockey puck-like spongecakes with sprayed-on whipped cream that too often pass for shortcake today. *"The shortcake I remember," said one of the men dreamily, "was like a biscuit and served warm, with butter and plenty of heavy cream."*

I, too, grew up savoring this old-fashioned, country-style of shortcake. The highlight of summer dinners, this glorious dessert came to the table on a large, round, blue-and-white Chinese porcelain platter: two layers of hot, buttered biscuit with bright red strawberries glistening between them and spilling over the top. Mother cut the shortcake into wedges, parceling out the errant berries, and passed around a pitcher of thick, yellow cream from our own Guernsey cows.

Although strawberry shortcake remains the national standard, other flavorful berries such as raspberries, nagoonberries, or thimbleberries, or a combination of berries, can be substituted (leave them whole). The contrast between the hot, crisp, buttered biscuit and the cold sweetened berries makes this dish especially good, so the shortcake must be served immediately upon assembly.

Slice or quarter the strawberries into a large bowl and add the sugar. Toss gently, adding more sugar to taste. Set the berries in the refrigerator to thoroughly chill, stirring occasionally so the sugar dissolves.

Preheat the oven to 425°F. Generously grease a 10-inch pie pan.

About 3 quarts strawberries, washed and hulled
1 cup sugar, more to taste
1/4 cup softened butter, for serving
Heavy cream, whipped cream, or Crème Fraîche (see page 47), for serving

For the shortcake biscuit, sift the flour, sugar, baking powder, and salt into a large mixing bowl. Cut in the shortening and work lightly with a pastry blender or your fingers until the mixture resembles coarse meal. Starting with 1 cup, add enough milk to form a soft dough, mixing lightly with a fork. Turn the dough onto a floured board and pat into a ball and then a circle. Place the dough in the pie pan and pat to fit. Bake until golden, about 15 minutes.

Remove the biscuit to a board and slice through the dough horizontally to form two layers. Use a pancake turner to flip the top layer onto a serving platter, cut side up. (The biscuit may crumble a bit—just press the crumbs back in place when assembling the shortcake.) Spread both halves with the softened butter. Spoon half the chilled strawberries onto the first biscuit layer, add the second layer, buttered side up, and top with the remaining berries. Serve immediately, with a pitcher of heavy cream or bowl of whipped cream or Crème Fraîche passed separately.

SHORTCAKE BISCUIT

3 cups all-purpose flour

3 tablespoons sugar

1 tablespoon baking powder

1 teaspoon salt

1/2 cup vegetable shortening

1 cup milk, more if needed

Makes 8 servings.

VARIATION: To make individual shortcakes, roll or pat the biscuit dough to a thickness of 3/4 inch, and cut out 8 rounds with a biscuit cutter. Place them on a greased baking sheet and bake 10 to 12 minutes, until golden. Split and butter the biscuits. To serve, place the bottom half of a biscuit on a plate, mound with sweetened berries, and cover with the top (buttered side down). Spoon additional berries around the shortcake.

Suzanne's Gingered Pear and Cranberry Cobbler

M y friend Suzanne Bishop lives in Fairbanks with her journalist husband, Sam, and their two small daughters, on a road with the enchanting name of Howling Dog Trail. A dedicated baker, she developed this sublime winter cobbler in her spare moments away from managing a fund-raising campaign for the University of Alaska Museum.

For the biscuit topping, combine the flour, sugar, and baking powder in a large bowl. Add the butter and cut in with a pastry blender or rub with your fingers until the mixture resembles coarse meal. In another bowl, beat the egg with the half-and-half and add to the flour mixture along with the ginger. Stir lightly with a fork, just to moisten the dough. Shape the dough into a ball and chill for at least 15 minutes.

Preheat the oven to 350°F.

Heat the cranberries with 2 tablespoons water in a saucepan for a few minutes until the berries begin to pop. Combine them with the pear slices, sugar, and lemon juice in an 8-inch square baking dish. Dot with the butter and place the dish in the oven for about 20 minutes or until the fruit starts to bubble.

Roll or pat the dough to fit the top of the baking dish. Place on top of the fruit and press the edges to the sides of the pan. Slash the dough in several places to vent steam.

Mix the sugar and the cinnamon and sprinkle over the dough, for topping. Return the pan to the oven for 10 to 15 minutes or until the crust is golden and fruit bubbles through the vents. Serve warm, with vanilla ice cream.

Makes 6 servings.

BISCUIT TOPPING
1 cup all-purpose flour
1/4 cup sugar
2 teaspoons baking powder
1/4 cup cold butter, cut into
  pieces
1 egg
1/4 cup half-and-half
2 tablespoons finely chopped
  crystallized ginger

FILLING
1 cup cranberries
2 1/2 pounds fresh pears,
  peeled, cored, and cut into
  1/4-inch slices (about 4 cups)
1/4 cup sugar
2 tablespoons lemon juice
2 tablespoons butter

TOPPING
2 tablespoons sugar
1/2 teaspoon ground
  cinnamon
Vanilla ice cream, for serving

Rhubarb Crisp

In summer, Alaskans move at a hectic pace, cramming the lengthening days with as many activities as possible. Social events tend toward spur-of-the-moment outdoor affairs like beach picnics and barbecues. Humble crumbles, or crisps, come into their own on these occasions. Quickly assembled of fresh or frozen fruits, they can be doubled or tripled to feed a crowd, transport handily, and taste wonderful served warm or cold. No dessert could be more typically Alaskan than this simple rhubarb crisp.

Preheat the oven to 375°F. Grease a 9-inch square baking pan.

Stir together the rhubarb with the sugar, flour, and nutmeg and spread in the prepared pan. (When using young, juicy rhubarb, you may need to increase the flour slightly.)

To make the streusel topping, combine the flour and sugar in a mixing bowl. Cut in the butter with a pastry blender or two knives until the mixture resembles coarse meal (or use a food processor). Add the walnuts and sprinkle the streusel over the rhubarb. Bake for 45 minutes to 1 hour (about 15 minutes longer if using frozen rhubarb), until the filling bubbles around the edges of the topping and the streusel has browned.

Makes 8 to 10 servings.

6 cups diced rhubarb
1 cup sugar
2 1/2 tablespoons all-purpose flour
1/2 teaspoon ground nutmeg

STREUSEL TOPPING
1 cup all-purpose flour
1 cup sugar
1/2 cup cold butter, cut into pieces
1 cup coarsely chopped walnuts

Apple Cranberry Cardamom Crisp

*T*he sweet-tart combination of apples and cranberries shows up in many North Country desserts. In this example, cardamom, the favorite Scandinavian baking spice, lends an exotic touch to a satisfying fall crisp.

Preheat the oven to 375°F. Grease an 8-inch square baking pan.

Toss together the apple slices, cranberries, sugar, lemon juice, and cardamom and place in the prepared pan.

For the streusel topping, mix the flour and brown sugar and cut in the butter with a pastry blender or two knives (or use a food processor). Add the oats and nuts, and spread the streusel evenly over the fruit mixture. Bake for 1 hour, or until the streusel browns and the fruit juices bubble around the edges of the pan.

Makes 8 servings.

5 cups peeled, cored, and
   sliced tart apples (about
   5 medium apples)
1 cup cranberries
1/2 cup sugar
2 tablespoons lemon juice
1/2 teaspoon ground
   cardamom

STREUSEL TOPPING
2/3 cup all-purpose flour
2/3 cup firmly packed
   brown sugar
1/3 cup butter
1/3 cup rolled oats
1/3 cup coarsely chopped
   walnuts or pecans

Custards and Puddings

Sacks Café Dark Chocolate Pots de Crème

Those who know chocolate know Anchorage's Sacks Café, which JoAnn Asher and Margie Brown opened in November 1983. In addition to such enticing concoctions as Scallop and Crab Cakes with Honey Chipotle Aïoli and Apple-Smoked Beef Tenderloin with Roasted Onions and Green Peppercorn Brandy Demi-Glace, their eclectic "New American Cuisine" menu offers two signature desserts: a flourless Chocolate Gâteau and these ultra-rich Dark Chocolate Pots de Crème. Generously endowed with bittersweet chocolate and Triple Sec, they elevate the plebeian custard into something approaching art.

Preheat the oven to 300°F. Put on a kettle of water to boil.

Break the chocolate into chunks and put them in the top of a double boiler with the cream. Heat the mixture, stirring occasionally, until the chocolate melts, but do not allow it to boil. In a large bowl, whisk the egg yolks and sugar until well mixed. Gradually blend in the chocolate mixture, vanilla, and liqueur.

Divide the mixture into 12 custard cups and place them in a roasting pan. Add boiling water to reach halfway up the sides of the cups and bake for about 1 hour, or until just set. Chill the custards. Just before serving, pipe a swirl of whipped cream on the top of each custard and sprinkle with chocolate shavings.

Makes 12 servings.

12 ounces bittersweet baking chocolate
1 quart heavy cream
12 egg yolks
3/4 cup sugar
1 1/2 tablespoons vanilla extract
1/4 cup Triple Sec or other orange-flavored liqueur
Whipped cream and shaved chocolate, for serving

Barbara's Baked Vanilla Custard

My y mother's custard can only be described as silken. Her secrets: strain the mixture before baking, and cook it slowly and not too long. Baked custards should still quiver slightly in the center when removed from the oven. This basic formula produces a soft, delicate custard, the ultimate comfort food.

Preheat the oven to 325°F. Put on a kettle of water to boil.

Beat the eggs lightly with a fork. Add the sugar and salt and continue beating with the fork until blended. Blend in the milk and vanilla, and strain the mixture into 6 small custard cups or a 1-quart baking dish. Sprinkle generously with cinnamon.

Place the custard cups or baking dish in a larger baking pan, and add boiling water to reach halfway up the sides of the dish(es). Bake until a knife inserted into the custard comes out clean, about 40 minutes for small custards and 50 minutes for a large one. Remove the custard from the hot water bath and allow to cool before serving.

Makes 4 to 6 servings.

2 eggs
1/2 cup sugar
Pinch of salt
2 cups milk
1 teaspoon vanilla extract
Ground cinnamon, for topping

RICH CUSTARD VARIATION: Add 2 egg yolks to the whole eggs.

COFFEE CUSTARD VARIATION: Heat the milk with 2 to 3 tablespoons of ground coffee and let stand to infuse for 10 to 15 minutes. Strain the milk into the egg and sugar mixture. Omit the cinnamon topping.

Ginger Cup Custards

The crystallized ginger in these enriched custards provides a warm glow on the frostiest of Alaskan evenings. Serve them beside the fire at a winter party, with Fiddlehead Ginger Crinkles (see page 25).

Preheat the oven to 325°F. Put on a kettle of water to boil.

Place the crystallized ginger, sugar, and salt in the bowl of a food processor and process to pulverize the ginger (or chop finely by hand); set aside. Beat the eggs and egg yolks with a fork. Add the milk and vanilla, and beat until blended. Strain the mixture into the food processor bowl containing the ginger-sugar mix, and pulse until blended. Pour into 6 small custard cups and dust generously with cinnamon and ginger.

Place the cups in a larger baking pan and add boiling water to reach halfway up the sides of the dishes. Bake until a knife inserted into the custard comes out clean, about 40 minutes. The center of the custard should still quiver slightly. Remove the custards from the hot water bath and allow to cool before serving.

Makes 6 servings.

3 or 4 slices crystallized ginger
1/2 cup sugar
Pinch of salt
2 whole eggs
2 egg yolks
2 cups milk
1/2 teaspoon vanilla extract
Ground cinnamon and ginger, for topping

Clinkerdagger's Burnt Cream

The Anchorage branch of Clinkerdagger's, a former Northwest restaurant chain, hooked a generation of Alaskans on this English classic of egg yolks and cream with a broiled sugar topping (known also as crème brûlée). Thanks to their printed recipe cards, the dessert lives on.

Preheat the oven to 325°F. Put on a kettle of water to boil.

Heat the cream over moderate heat until nearing the boiling point, and set aside. In a medium bowl, beat the egg yolks and sugar together until thick and creamy. Slowly add the cream, whisking constantly, and blend well. Add the vanilla and strain the mixture into 6 individual custard cups that can withstand the direct heat of the broiler.

Place the custard cups in a baking pan and fill the pan with boiling water to reach halfway up the sides of the dishes. Bake until a knife inserted into the custard comes out clean, about 40 minutes. Remove the custards from the water bath, cool to room temperature, then chill thoroughly.

For the caramelized topping, spread 1 to 2 teaspoons of granulated sugar over the top of each chilled custard. Place the custards directly under the broiler for about 3 minutes until the sugar bubbles and turns golden.

Makes 6 servings.

2 cups heavy cream
4 egg yolks
1/2 cup sugar
1 tablespoon vanilla extract
Granulated sugar for
   caramelized topping

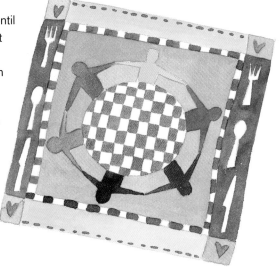

Kachemak Bay Wilderness Lodge Berry Rhubarb Bread Pudding

A feeling of renewal envelops you at Kachemak Bay Wilderness Lodge, Diane and Michael McBride's hand-hewn log sanctuary on the Kenai Peninsula in Southcentral Alaska, a 30-minute boat ride from Homer. Here, amid the spectacle of 28-foot tides, moss-hung conifers, eagle nests, and wildflowers, you can reacquaint yourself with the primal rhythms of the planet.

Meanwhile, the staff will be attending to more pedestrian concerns, such as emptying crab pots, filleting salmon, and baking the daily bread. Diane often combines leftover white, whole wheat, and oat bread to make this Alaska-style bread pudding. Any kind of berry, or a combination of them, can be used in this pudding, but raspberries make an especially appealing dish. Toasting the bread cubes enhances the flavor as well as the texture.

Preheat the oven to 350°F. Grease a 9-by-13-inch baking pan.

Spread the toasted bread cubes in the prepared pan. Beat the eggs until foamy. Beat in 1/2 cup of the sugar, the milk, vanilla, and cinnamon and pour the mixture over the bread cubes. Stir in the berries and rhubarb. Distribute the remaining 1/4 cup of sugar over the top and sprinkle on the nutmeg. Bake 30 to 45 minutes, until firm and crusty around the edges. Serve warm, perhaps garnished with a few fresh berries.

Makes 8 servings.

4 cups 1-inch bread cubes, toasted
3 eggs
3/4 cup sugar
3 cups milk
1 teaspoon vanilla extract
1/2 teaspoon ground cinnamon
1 cup berries, more for garnish if desired
1/2 cup diced rhubarb
1/2 teaspoon ground nutmeg, for topping

Lemon Puff Pudding

*L*emon provides the perfect finish to a meal of salmon or halibut, often the main dish of choice for Alaskans cooking at home. Known by various names—including lemon sponge custard and lemon pudding cake—this timeless dessert separates while baking to form a delicate, puffy sponge cake on top of a brisk lemon sauce. In berry season, I like to serve the pudding chilled, with a spoonful of Fresh Raspberry Sauce (see page 95).

Preheat the oven to 325°F. Put on a kettle of water to boil.

Cream the butter with 1/2 cup of the sugar and the flour. Add the egg yolks and beat well. Stir in the milk, lemon juice, and lemon zest. In another bowl, beat the egg whites and salt until they reach soft peaks. Gradually beat in the remaining 1/2 cup sugar and fold the meringue into the lemon mixture. Pour into a 1 1/2-quart soufflé dish or other decorative baking dish and place the dish in a larger baking pan. Add boiling water to reach halfway up the sides of the baking dish. Bake the pudding for 1 hour, until puffed and golden. Dust with powdered sugar before serving warm or cold.

Makes 6 servings.

3 tablespoons butter
1 cup sugar
1/4 cup all-purpose flour
3 eggs, separated
1 1/2 cups milk
1/4 cup lemon juice
2 teaspoons grated lemon zest
1/4 teaspoon salt
Powdered sugar, for dusting

Ozark Pudding

In the 1940s, housewives across Alaska and the Lower 48 learned Bess Truman's recipe for Ozark Pudding, said to be President Harry Truman's favorite dessert. The crunchy mixture of apples, walnuts, and sugar, lightly bound with eggs and a little flour— more a torte than a pudding—still wins plenty of votes from backcountry bakers. Assembled in minutes with a whisk and a wooden spoon, this delicious, unfussy dessert cooks perfectly in a woodstove.

Preheat the oven to 325°F. Lightly grease a 10-inch round or 9-inch square baking pan.

Beat the eggs well with a whisk. Add the sugar and vanilla, and continue beating until light and creamy. Sift together the flour, baking powder, and salt and stir into the egg mixture. Fold in the apples and nuts.

Spread the batter into the baking pan and bake for 35 to 40 minutes, until the top looks brown and crusty. Serve the pudding warm, with unsweetened whipped cream.

Makes 8 to 10 servings.

2 eggs
1 1/2 cups sugar
2 teaspoons vanilla extract
2/3 cup all-purpose flour
2 1/2 teaspoons baking powder
1/4 teaspoon salt
1 cup coarsely chopped peeled apples
1 cup coarsely chopped walnuts
Unsweetened whipped cream, for serving

Baked Alaska and

Other Frozen Desserts

Baked Alaska Hotel Captain Cook

Joe Hickel, pastry chef at the Hotel Captain Cook, has presided over the Anchorage dessert scene for more than 20 years, turning out handmade French pastries, ices, and silky chocolate decadence, not to mention the annual 9-by-12-foot gingerbread village for the hotel's Christmas window. His delightfully unorthodox version of Baked Alaska, the showy construction of cold ice cream and hot meringue (reputedly invented by an American physicist in the 19th century) combines coffee ice cream, caramel, and raspberry sauce on a flourless chocolate brownie base, topped with meringue rosettes. For that final touch, Joe browns the meringues with a propane torch.

Preheat the oven to 375°F. Lightly oil a 9-inch springform pan.

Cream the butter until light. Gradually add the sugar and continue creaming until very light and fluffy. Add the eggs one at a time, beating well after each, then add the vanilla. Blend in the chocolate and pecans. Pour the batter into the pan, smooth the top, and bake for about 35 minutes, or until a wooden toothpick shows moist crumbs. Cool in the pan to room temperature; do not unmold. During baking the brownie will probably form a crisp upper layer that separates from the rest of the cake; press it down onto the top of the cake.

To make the caramel sauce, heat the cream until steaming but not boiling and set aside. Place the sugar in a heavy-bottomed sauté or frying pan and cook over medium heat, stirring with a wooden spoon, until the sugar melts and turns amber. Remove the pan from the heat and pour the hot cream into the melted sugar, while continuing to stir. Take extreme care during this operation because the caramelized sugar will bubble furiously when you add the cream. Return the pan to the heat and stir the mixture until thoroughly melted and combined. Transfer the sauce to a stainless steel bowl to cool.

Chocolate Pecan Brownie Base

6 tablespoons unsalted butter

1 cup sugar

4 eggs

1 teaspoon vanilla extract

1 cup semisweet chocolate chips, melted and slightly cooled

1/2 cup pecan pieces

1/4 cup raspberry jam, for topping

2 quarts Coffee Ice Cream (see page 86), for topping

Caramel Sauce

2/3 cup heavy cream

3/4 cup sugar

Spread the cooled brownie base with a thin layer of caramel sauce followed by the raspberry jam, smearing the jam into the caramel. Remove the ice cream from the freezer until softened enough to spread. Pack the ice cream on top of the cake, smoothing to the edges of the pan. Cover with plastic wrap and foil and freeze for several hours, until completely solid.

Just before serving, make the meringue: Beat the egg whites until frothy. Add the vanilla and cream of tartar and continue beating on high speed until soft peaks form. Reduce the speed to medium and beat in the sugar a spoonful or two at a time. Return to high speed and continue beating until the eggs whites are glossy and fairly stiff but not dry. Remove the cake from the freezer, unwrap, and place on a chilled serving platter. Using a pastry bag with a large star tip, pipe a meringue rosette on top of each serving and quickly brown them with a propane torch. Or, pipe the rosettes onto a lightly oiled sheet of parchment paper or foil and bake them at 350°F until golden, then transfer them quickly to the top of the cake. Wet a dish towel with hot water, wring out, and apply briefly to the outer ring of the pan. Release and remove the ring and serve the Baked Alaska with the remaining caramel sauce.

MERINGUE (see note below)
2 egg whites
1/2 teaspoon vanilla extract
1/8 teaspoon cream of tartar
1/4 cup powdered sugar

Makes 8 servings.

A Cautionary Note Due to the possible presence of harmful salmonella bacteria in raw or undercooked eggs, USDA safety guidelines specify cooking eggs to an internal temperature of 160°F and baking a meringue for 15 minutes at 350°F. However, you should always consider yourself at risk when consuming such foods. Very high-risk individuals, including children, the elderly, and those suffering from immune-deficiency disorders, should probably avoid them altogether.

Coffee Ice Cream

In the stereotypical image of Alaska, a battered tin coffeepot steams over a prospector's campfire or atop the woodstove of a sourdough's cabin. Truth imitates fiction in this instance. Alaskans never stray far from the bitter brew, whether thick pottery mugs of "joe," Styrofoam cups of latte, or a rich coffee ice cream.

Combine the milk, cream, and coffee in a heavy-bottomed saucepan and place over moderate heat. Heat, stirring occasionally, until steaming but not boiling. Meanwhile, whisk the egg yolks in a medium mixing bowl. Gradually whisk in the sugar. Beating constantly, strain the hot mixture into the egg yolks and sugar, starting with a dribble and increasing the volume as the egg yolks warm. Stir in the vanilla.

2 cups milk
2 cups heavy cream
1/4 cup ground coffee
6 egg yolks
1 cup sugar
2 teaspoons vanilla extract

Rinse the saucepan. Return the mixture to the pan and cook over low to moderate heat, stirring constantly, until the mixture thickens enough to coat the back of a wooden spoon. Cool to room temperature and refrigerate. Transfer the chilled base to an ice cream maker and freeze as directed.

Makes 8 servings.

QUICK COFFEE ICE CREAM VARIATION: Soften 2 quarts of good-quality vanilla ice cream and place in a large mixing bowl. Blend in 1 tablespoon of instant espresso powder (more to taste). Pack into a storage container and return to the freezer until firm.

Luscious Fresh Blueberry Sorbet

No dessert so captures the fresh flavors and jewel-like colors of Alaska's berries as sorbets. And with a simple hand-operated ice cream maker such as the Donvier, which employs a prefrozen cylinder of coolant instead of cracked ice and salt, these beautiful fruit ices require little advance planning and practically no time at all to make. This mixture of simple sugar syrup and pureed raw blueberries produces a luscious purple-blue ice with a surprising cherry flavor.

Puree the blueberries in a food processor. Add 1 cup of the cold sugar syrup, the lemon juice, and salt and process until well blended. Transfer the mixture to an ice cream maker and freeze as directed. Pack the sorbet in a plastic container and firm in the freezer before serving.

3 cups fresh blueberries
1 cup cold Sugar Syrup
  (see recipe below)
Juice of 1 lemon
1/8 teaspoon salt

Makes 6 to 8 servings.

Sugar Syrup

2 1/2 cups sugar
2 cups boiling water

Put the sugar in a heatproof jar or bowl, add the boiling water, and stir until the sugar dissolves. Chill thoroughly—the syrup must be cold for making sorbet. Covered and refrigerated, the sugar syrup will keep for several weeks.

Makes about 3 1/2 cups.

Strawberry Rhubarb Sorbet

A laskan cooks find all sorts of uses for the ubiquitous rhubarb, the pride of every amateur gardener, which succeeds in the most unlikely conditions. Its unique tart flavor makes a wonderful fruit ice. Used alone, rhubarb ranges in color from deep red to greenish pink, so this formula includes just enough strawberries to enhance the color of the sorbet without overpowering the flavor of the rhubarb. Sensational with Vanilla Sour Cream Gelato (see page 90).

Place the rhubarb in a saucepan with 3 tablespoons water and simmer slowly, covered, until tender. Chill for at least 1 hour. Transfer the contents of the saucepan to the bowl of a food processor, add the strawberries and syrup, and process for 30 seconds. Scrape down the sides of the bowl, add the lemon juice, and continue processing for another 30 seconds or until uniformly pureed. Add additional lemon juice to taste.

3 cups diced rhubarb
1 cup hulled, washed, and chilled strawberries
2 cups cold sugar syrup (see page 87)
Juice of 1 lemon, plus more to taste

Transfer the mixture to an ice cream maker and freeze as directed. Pack the sorbet in a plastic container and firm in the freezer before serving.

Makes 8 to 10 servings.

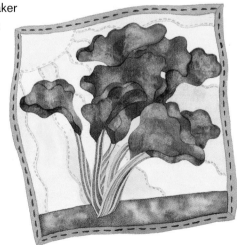

Cranberry Orange Ice

*F*lavorful low-bush cranberries, also called lingonberries, flourish in forests and tundra throughout Alaska and can be used interchangeably with the domestic variety. The basic formula for this ice comes from a 1946 cookbook compiled by the Ladies Aid Society of the Federated Church of Nome. I reduced the sugar and brightened the mixture with orange juice and seltzer. Pink and citrusy, the ice can stand alone as a light dessert or freshen the palate between courses of a holiday dinner.

In a small saucepan, cook the cranberries in the water until the skins pop. Pass them through a sieve to remove the skins, pressing with the back of a spoon to capture as much pulp as possible. Stir the sugar and orange juice into the cranberry puree, and chill the mixture for several hours or overnight. Add the seltzer water and lemon juice to taste.

Transfer the mixture to an ice cream maker and freeze as directed. Pack the ice in a plastic container and firm in the freezer before serving.

Makes 6 to 8 servings.

2 cups cranberries
1 cup water
1 cup sugar
1/2 cup orange juice
3/4 cup chilled plain seltzer water
Juice of 1 lemon, plus more to taste

Vanilla Sour Cream Gelato

*F*or a few heady years, Juneau enjoyed the services of a small French bakery–cafe owned by a very hardworking husband-and-wife team. Sadly, the Loatmans escaped across the Pacific to reveal the mysteries of baguette-making to Japanese bakers. In addition to bread, croissants, pastries, and chocolates, Le Petit Paris offered handmade sorbets and ice creams, including an admirable lighter-style vanilla sour cream gelato. Their concoction probably started with a proper custard base, but this simple formula produces delicious results. Serve alone or with a fresh fruit sauce (see pages 94-95).

Chill the ingredients before beginning. Whisk all of the ingredients together. Transfer the mixture to an ice cream maker and freeze as directed. Pack the gelato in a plastic container and firm in the freezer before serving.

Makes 4 servings.

1 cup sour cream
1 cup half-and-half
1/2 cup sugar
2 teaspoons vanilla extract
Pinch of salt

Cantaloupe Gelato

In Alaska I developed a deep appreciation for cantaloupes. While soft summer fruits often arrive in markets bruised and bedraggled from their long journey north, these useful melons remain dependably sound, ready to be packed off to even more remote locales by floatplane, kayak, or skiff. This easy-to-make gelato preserves the ripe cantaloupe flavor.

Chill all of the ingredients before beginning. Puree the cantaloupe in a food processor. Add the sugar and lemon juice and process to blend. Stir in the cream, milk, vanilla, and additional lemon juice to taste. Transfer the mixture to an ice cream maker and freeze as directed. Pack the gelato into a plastic container and firm in the freezer before serving.

Makes 4 to 6 servings.

1 cup diced cantaloupe pulp
1/3 cup sugar
1 teaspoon lemon juice, plus
   more to taste
1/2 cup heavy cream
1/2 cup milk
1/4 teaspoon vanilla extract

Crystal Snow Jenne's Lemon Sherbet

The Juneau Centennial Cookbook *includes this recipe from Corrinne Jenne Kenway. Corrinne's mother, Crystal Snow Jenne, arrived in Alaska with her parents in 1887 and traveled over the Chilkoot Pass with them at age ten, in 1894. She graduated in the second class of the Juneau High School and later taught school in Juneau.*

The Jenne family liked to take their ice cream freezer to the Mendenhall Glacier for a picnic lunch, pack the freezer with rock salt and glacier ice, and take turns cranking the dessert. This recipe results in a smooth-textured milk sherbet with a wonderful, fresh flavor—even without glacier ice.

Start with cold ingredients for best results. In a medium bowl, stir together the sugar and lemon juice. Slowly add the milk and cream, stirring constantly (don't worry if mixture appears curdled). Taste for tartness, adding more sugar or lemon juice to taste.

Transfer the mixture to an ice cream maker and freeze as directed. Pack the sherbet into a plastic container and firm in the freezer before serving.

Makes 8 servings.

1 1/2 cups sugar, more to taste
Juice of 3 lemons (about 2/3 cup), more to taste
2 cups milk
2 cups heavy cream

Simon & Seafort's Brandy Ice

*P*ractically everyone in Alaska knows about the high-octane shakes from Simon & Seafort's Restaurant in Anchorage. The "adult milkshakes" have been a dessert fixture since opening day, when they demonstrated their popularity by burning out a succession of bar mixers. Twenty years later, Simon & Seafort's whips up 90 gallons of Brandy Ice a week in summer, using the big mixers in the back. Best to save these for the end of the day.

Combine the ice cream, brandy, Kahlua, and crème de cacao in a milkshake can or blender jar, and whip at medium speed until smooth but still very thick. Serve in tall glasses.

Makes 2 servings.

1 1/2 cups good-quality vanilla
   ice cream
2 tablespoons brandy
2 teaspoons Kahlua
2 teaspoons dark crème
   de cacao

FRESH FRUIT SAUCES

Fresh fruit or berry sauce served warm over vanilla ice cream proves that simplest can be best. Such sauces defy precise formulas, the results depending upon whether the fruits are wild or cultivated, fresh or frozen, tart or sweet, and juicy or not. Consider these recipes a starting point and adjust to suit.

Fresh Blueberry Sauce

M ost recipes for blueberry sauce start by cooking the berries with water. I find this dilutes the flavor, and add water only if the berries aren't very juicy.

Mix the blueberries, sugar, and cornstarch in a heavy saucepan and place over medium-low heat. Add the lemon juice and stir gently while the sugar dissolves and the berries gradually release their juice. (Add 1 tablespoon of water if necessary to get them started.) Simmer very gently until the sauce thickens slightly, about 5 minutes, then adjust the flavor and consistency with additional sugar, lemon juice, or water. Cultivated berries generally require a bit more lemon than their wild cousins.

2 cups blueberries
1/4 cup sugar
1 teaspoon cornstarch
1 tablespoon lemon juice

Makes about 1 1/2 cups.

BLUEBERRY RIPPLE ICE CREAM: Sieve Blueberry Sauce to remove the skins. Swirl the puree into softened vanilla ice cream, and refreeze until firm.

Fresh Rhubarb Sauce

*S*erve this sauce warm with Vanilla Sour Cream Gelato (see page 90) or other vanilla-flavored ice cream or frozen yogurt.

Simmer the rhubarb, sugar, and water for 10 to 15 minutes, or until tender. Adjust to taste with additional sugar, water, or lemon juice to achieve the desired sweetness and consistency. Makes about 2 cups.

2 cups diced rhubarb
1/2 cup sugar
1/4 cup water
Lemon juice

Fresh Raspberry Sauce

*A*mong the most useful and beautiful of dessert sauces, Fresh Raspberry Sauce provides a finishing touch to cakes such as Chocolate Almond Torte (see page 46) and Lemon Pound Cake (see page 40), ice creams, or fresh fruit. You can substitute strawberries for all or part of the raspberries.

Sieve the berries to remove the seeds, and transfer the puree to an electric blender. Add the sugar and lemon juice and blend at medium-high speed for 30 seconds. Taste, adding additional lemon juice and sugar as needed. Blend in the optional liqueur and refrigerate until serving.

Makes about 1 1/2 cups.

2 cups raspberries
3 tablespoons sugar,
   more to taste
1 tablespoon lemon
   juice, more to taste
1 to 2 tablespoons
   kirsch, Cognac, or
   orange-flavored liqueur
   (optional)

Index